Keller's OUTDOOR SURVIVAL Guide

HOW TO PREVAIL WHEN LOST, STRANDED, OR INJURED IN THE WILDERNESS

BY WILLIAM KELLER

WILLOW CREEK PRESS

Minocqua, Wisconsin

Published by Willow Creek Press
P.O. Box 147
Minocqua, Wisconsin 54548

For information on other Willow Creek Press titles, call 1-800-850-9453

Edited by Andrea Donner
Designed by Patricia Bickner Linder

Library of Congress Cataloging-in-Publication Data
    Keller, William, 1956-
        [Outdoor survival guide]
        Keller's outdoor survival guide : how to prevail when lost, stranded, or injured in the wilderness / by William Keller.
            p. cm. -- (Willow Creek Guides)
    Includes index.
        ISBN 1-57223266-8 (pbk. : alk. paper)
        1. Wilderness survival--Handbooks, manuals, etc. I. Title: Outdoor survival guide.
    II. Title. III. Series.
        GV200.5 .K42 2001
        613.6'9--dc21   2001005245

Printed in Canada

This book is dedicated to all volunteer and professional rescuers and their families. The public often fails to appreciate the time involvement, responsibilities, stress, and sacrifice these people routinely make. Though the victims often fail to provide a simple thank-you, your services and dedication are invaluable.

Contents

Preface

In twenty years of involvement with search-and-rescue and emergency services in Colorado and Nebraska, I've been involved in hundreds of search missions and hundreds of rescue missions—for lost or injured hunters, hikers, fishermen, children, elderly, disabled, and mentally-impaired people. I've seen the aftermath of aircraft crashes, lightning fatalities, gunshot accidents, stab injuries, car accidents, four-wheeler accidents, horse-riding injuries, sudden storms, avalanches, drowning, and many other calamities. I have been involved in several missions that involved rescuing animals including dogs and horses.

I have learned many of the survival techniques by my own mistakes in the wilderness. I have personally experienced being lost, cold, injured and hungry. I have experienced hypothermia, broken bones, serious cuts and even a gunshot wound in my upper leg as a result of a hunting accident.

In this book, along with practical survival techniques, I have provided personal stories of search and rescue missions so you can learn from those who made good decisions, those who were fortunate, and those whose fortune ran out. It is my wish that reading this book will offer insight into how quickly a day of casual recreation can turn into a life or death situation. I hope that after reading this book, you will never enter remote areas without a basic survival kit and greater knowledge of how to handle yourself when the worst-case scenario actually occurs. And it is my sincere goal that this book may actually save someone's life — or at least improve their chances. I hope you enjoy and benefit from the information.

Survival:
A State of Mind

One mid-winter evening about 7 PM we received a call for a 25-30 year old, lost cross-country skier. The subject had gotten separated from the other skiers, and not returned to the vehicle as planned. This person had decided to go into areas that exceeded the ability of the rest of the group, all of whom wisely chose not to follow him.

The group had intended to ski an area that was not very difficult, but it had some "sucker holes"—areas that are known to draw skiers into them but are extremely difficult to ski out of. These areas have a history of searches with similar outcomes, due to the victims' typical reactions.

We had some exceptionally talented cross-country skiers in our group. One of our best skiers was named Jeff. He skied these areas often and knew them well. Jeff liked to ski alone on this type of mission because few other skiers could keep up with him. It is very risky to send a person in alone, but Jeff was equipped with a radio in case he got into trouble.

Jeff was an EMT and an expert in wilderness survival. He carried minimal equipment, but he had the ability to camp with the victim or to support him as necessary. Jeff also had the means and experience to warm a person safely—as well as anyone can in a wilderness setting.

This particular search started with tracks heading into a known sucker hole. Jeff followed the tracks from the last known point, continually advising us of the direction of travel. Everything indicated that this skier had dropped into a known area and that Jeff would soon overtake the lost person, point him in the right direction, and bring him out.

Then we heard from Jeff that the tracks were not going into the normal sucker hole area, but had gone into a new area. This track dropped over into a very steep, thick-brush area that is practically impossible for even the best skier to maneuver. I had hiked that area during the summer months and I knew it would be difficult to ski on this dark night. Jeff was using a headlamp to navigate. It was the brush that would cause the greatest problems for him. He could handle the steep inclines, but the branches and tree limbs would be all through the snow, tripping him.

Jeff dropped over the top, following the track down. The search command post understood what he was getting into and sent in second and third teams for backup. The backup teams were being transported to the ridge by snowmobiles pulling rescue sleds, blankets and other equipment. We were confident that our skier would not be far. We also called for an ambulance to stand by at the command post, assuming the skier was injured, and in case one of our own became injured.

Jeff had skied down over the ridge only about 75 yards from the top when he found the skier. The man was next to a tree, in a fetal position, incoherent, and only semi-conscious. He had thrashed around and melted a hole through three feet of snow down to the ground with his body heat. He was on the frozen ground, curled up in a ball, and in a hole in the snow.

He was dangerously hypothermic and very near death. He had not been injured, but was suffering as a result of the exposure. The skier had gone into an area so difficult he was unable to get back out. Unable to help himself, he panicked and lost control mentally. He had given up any hope and was in the process of dying. He would not have survived another hour. The rescuers could see that he had tried unsuccessfully to start a fire by burning all his cash and other papers in his wallet.

A person in this condition is extremely fragile. EMT training even prevents the use of an airway on a hypothermia patient because activating the gag reflex can cause the person to go into cardiac arrest. The slightest movement, the slightest exertion, can cause death because of the tremendous strain on the body.

Jeff and the other rescuers now joining him had to make a decision: either move the patient as quickly as possible, knowing it would be many hours before reaching the ambulance, or attempt to warm the patient, stabilize his condition, and then attempt the transport.

Jeff and the other rescuers decided to warm the patient before attempting the move. A large fire was made nearby. The victim began to respond immediately, becoming more and more alert. His recovery may have been a combination of the heat from the fire and his realization that help had arrived.

Once a person is capable of swallowing on their own, they can be given warm fluids to drink. This will get warmth to the core of the body in the most efficient manner possible. It can be determined whether a person is alert enough to swallow by whether they are capable of holding a cup on their own. If they are alert enough to hold the cup, they will be able to drink fluids without choking. Once a person is taking warm fluids, the recovery process becomes much faster.

He was dangerously hypothermic and very near death. He had not been injured, but was suffering as a result of the exposure.

It took several hours before the rescuers felt the patient was ready to transport. Once they were comfortable the patient was warm enough, he was packed into a sled similar to those used by ski patrol.

It was determined that the fastest and most efficient direction would be to take the patient down instead of trying to climb back up to the top. By going down the face of the hill they would be right on top of the highway and the waiting ambulance.

Jeff guided the sled while other rescuers broke a trail and otherwise helped maneuver the load. Ropes were used to lower the load slowly, often using trees to wrap around and brake the descent. It was 10 AM the following morning when the exhausted rescue team broke out of the trees and onto the road with the patient. The patient was loaded into the ambulance and transported to the local hospital.

This is a good example of how much effort is put into a rescue. The rescuers all have day jobs, and all of the individuals involved on this mission had already put in a full day of work. They had gone without sleep since 6 or 7 AM the day prior. This means that they were operating in severe sleep deprivation having gone about 28-30 hours without sleep. The rescue work is exhausting, and now another day had started. They would either go to their jobs without sleep, or miss a day of work.

As for the patient, the rescuers had warmed him, the doctors had finished bringing him up to temperature, treated him for minor frostbite, and checked him out. He did not have any other injuries and would make a full recovery; in fact, he was out of the hospital by late that afternoon.

Are the people we rescue always grateful? This person never said "Thank you" or expressed one word of gratitude. Two days following the rescue, I received a call from him, threatening to sue Search and Rescue and all the parties involved because we "negligently" left his new skies on the side of the mountain. He demanded that we retrieve his skis or we would be paying for them. We did neither.

Are You Prepared?

If you have ever been in an emergency situation when the results of your actions made the difference as to whether you *really* lived or died, then you understand the type of survival discussed in this book. A car crash, being stranded on a remote highway, getting lost in a snow storm, facing a natural disaster, a gunshot wound while hunting, falling while rock climbing or mountain biking — all can become life-threatening situations when knowing what actions to take can save your own or someone else's life. Understanding your environment, your mental and physical limits, your creativity and resourcefulness, along with the basic survival skills and a little bravery will greatly increase your ability to survive.

In the modern world, we are rapidly losing basic survival skills as we become more dependent on technology and modern conveniences. Advanced equipment and better technology have made it possible for humans to go places and do things that were inaccessible to us not many years ago. The invention and availability of Global Positioning Systems (GPS) make it possible for even a novice to navigate to any point on earth and back again. Cell and satellite phones make it possible to communicate from literally any point on the planet, giving us a sense of security in locations we would have previously feared.

These and other modern conveniences, however, are softening our knowledge of basic survival skills. Technological improvements are wonderful as long as they are kept in proper perspective and we are able to retain the basic survival skills that have protected us through the ages, especially for those who venture into the wilderness to hike, hunt, mountain climb, camp, etc.

In order to determine your knowledge of basic survival skills, answer the following questions about how you would handle yourself in a remote wilderness setting:

- *If you became lost or stranded, what would you do?*
- *If you were driving your car and the engine quit on a remote road, it was cold and the heater no longer worked, what would you do?*
- *If you were lost, getting thirsty, and did not have any drinking water, would you know how to find a safe drink of water?*
- *Can you build a shelter to protect yourself from the elements?*
- *Can you build a fire?*
- *Can you build a fire in windy or wet conditions?*
- *Can you build a fire when your hands are cold and numb — so numb that you cannot hold a match or lighter?*
- *Do you know how to dry your clothing after a rain or if you have fallen into a stream?*
- *Would you recognize the symptoms of hypothermia in yourself or someone else before it was too late?*
- *Do you know how to warm yourself or a companion who is in a condition of hypothermia without causing further dangers, such as cardiac arrest?*
- *Do you know what you can and cannot eat in the wild?*
- *Do you know how to dress yourself for the conditions you will be exposed to? Will those clothes work if the conditions change?*
- *If you had a new GPS guidance system, what would you do if the batteries died or it was damaged and no longer worked?*
- *Do you have the ability to use a map and compass? Do you have a map and compass?*
- *Can you determine direction by the stars?*

If you have doubts as to what you would do in these situations, then you should spend some time learning survival techniques. The information in this book is not original, not difficult, nor is it everything you need to know to be a survival expert. It is simply time-tested, common-sense information that will put you in the right frame of mind to survive.

The ability to survive is prepared for in advance by planning and practice. The time to experiment with what does and does not work is in a controlled setting, not when your life depends on the results. For example, making a fire can be frustrating and difficult, but with proper technique and a little practice, it can be quite easy.

The best plan of action is to avoid dangerous situations. If this plan fails and you do get into trouble, having the knowledge, experience and means to deal with the problems you face will give you the best possible chance of survival.

Survival Basics

Ask several people to define the needs for a person to survive and you will get a variety of answers. The responses would be directly related to their past experiences and past exposures that they have considered as a threat to their life. An urban person might say "a Colt 45 and a credit card," while the country person might say "a shotgun and a knife," but most people will include air, food, water, clothing and shelter.

Every environment, whether urban, rural farmland, wilderness, range or desert, presents unique requirements for survival. These requirements are directly related to the amount of time you will be in that environment. Air, water, food, clothing and shelter account for the basic human needs, but the priority of those needs is unique to each situation depending on circumstances and time involvement.

A person can only go a few minutes without air, a few days without water, and a few weeks without food, but if you are in an environment in which you will freeze to death in minutes, then clothing and shelter become top priority. People in the Polar Bear Clubs dash out in the cold and jump into an icy lake for a minute or so, but they could not possibly survive if left in those conditions for any amount of time.

If you will be rescued in one hour and conditions are favorable, you will have very few needs. But if you will be required to spend one or several nights in a cold winter storm, you will have many needs.

Every survival situation is different, yet all have certain things in common. To be fully prepared, you must understand both the mechanics of survival—what you need physically—and the psychology of survival—the mentality you need to survive.

The Psychology of Survival: A Positive Mental Attitude

The single most important action you can perform in every survival situation is to *keep a positive mental attitude*. The ability to survive any situation is 80 percent mental, 10 percent equipment, 5 percent past experience and 5 percent chance or luck. If you keep your senses by maintaining a positive mental attitude and draw from past experiences, you can often compensate for the lack of equipment and greatly improve your chances.

In every emergency circumstance, you can increase your odds simply by maintaining a positive mental attitude. When you realize that you could die, remind yourself that you are *still* alive, and that *you can and will survive*.

A person can only go a few minutes without air, a few days without water, and a few weeks without food, but if you are in an environment in which you will freeze to death in minutes, then clothing and shelter become top priority.

Calm yourself down, talk to yourself if necessary, but keep your head. If you are afraid beyond any other experience in your life, think your way through the problem. The fear can enhance your senses and give you strength and endurance you may have never experienced before. Use those enhanced senses to generate resources and techniques that would normally never occur to you. If things get worse, don't give up. Treat it as another setback and go on. Make a personal resolve that you can and will survive this and anything else that happens until you are rescued. There is nothing more tragic than the person who held on through tremendous pain and effort only to give up just before help arrived.

There are countless books on the benefits of positive thinking, and it does work. You often hear stories of people who pulled through some traumatic injury or serious disease because they had "a will to live." On the other hand, you also hear of the person who died from an incident with minor injuries or minor medical problems "because they just gave up."

The mind is the most powerful survival tool you have. The human body can withstand pain and suffering that seems impossible to endure. I have rescued individuals who felt there was absolutely no hope of rescue, only to have a helicopter fly over the hill and pluck them from the situation. I have rescued individuals from conditions that I thought no one could possibly survive, and yet, those individuals escaped without any injury. In all my years with Search and Rescue, the most important lesson

I learned about survival is to *never underestimate a human's ability to survive*. In case after case, individuals who should have been body recoveries were found unscathed by the experience.

One case involved a man in his early fifties who got lost while hunting in a wilderness area. A winter storm set in that developed into an intense two-day blizzard. The man was described as 5'4", weighing 300 pounds. He was an insulin-dependent diabetic with extreme hypertension (high blood pressure) and in poor physical condition. The clothing he wore was made of cotton fabric, which is very poor for the wet conditions he was in. The amount of clothing he was wearing was not nearly enough for the temperatures or wind conditions.

The search command had established an area of high probability where he would be located. However, because of the terrain and weather conditions, we were unable to get there in a timely manner. Ground teams continued to make an effort but progress was slow and difficult. Helicopter support was the only real chance of getting to the man in a timely manner, but the weather kept us grounded.

Finally, the helicopter was able to lift off. The victim had by then spent 72 hours in the storm. Every searcher involved felt we were in for a body recovery. The helicopter flew into the search area and spotted the subject within five minutes. He was running out of the trees, waving his arms. This person had no injuries, no hypothermia, and no physical problems whatsoever as a result of his ordeal.

The helicopter is very limited at high elevations in regards to the amount of weight it can carry and still lift off. I loaded the victim in the chopper with the pilot so he could be flown to base. While waiting for the helicopter to return, I went through the victim's camp to see just what he had done to survive.

This person had survived quite comfortably through some of the worst conditions a person could be in. The man realized he was lost and that a storm was moving in quickly. Instead of wandering aimlessly, he stopped and looked for a place to camp. Luckily, he came across the remains of an old elk hunting camp that was in the trees and out of the wind. The previous hunters had left a lot of trash, including a couple of pieces of plastic, an old can of white gas lantern fuel that had about a cup left, some old cords and rope scraps, and an empty whiskey bottle. The victim fashioned a lean-to shelter that was fairly wind and water-resistant, and built a fire on the front edge. He used the whiskey bottle to melt snow by keeping it near the fire and pressing snow into it. He had some jerky and candy with him, and was relatively comfortable.

The most important thing this person did was maintain a positive mental attitude and keep his wits. Thinking through his situation, he determined his needs and found ways to fulfill them as well as he could.

Later that day, we returned to our rescue base only to be paged out for a lost cross-country skier. This person was described as being in his late twenties, in excellent health, excellent physique, and wearing high-quality windproof, waterproof clothing. The storm had passed and the weather was overcast, but very calm and much warmer, in the 20-degree range. The person was reported as having a fanny pack with some gear. Normally, based on the information given, we would give the person a little time to come in on their own, which would usually happen.

Our Search and Rescue teams had all of the equipment out for the previous search and, since the helicopter was still available, we decided to respond immediately. We flew into the area and picked up the lost skier's tracks from the air within thirty minutes.

The helicopter spotters are very experienced trackers and can tell a lot about the condition of the person by the tracks they leave. It was obvious that this person was in serious trouble. As hypothermia overtakes a person, they begin to lose mental ability, eventually beginning to hallucinate. They will often get feelings of claustrophobia and start discarding clothes and packs. This person had traveled about two miles when we overtook him. He was extremely hypothermic, had discarded his coat and shirt, and was wearing only his shoes and snow pants. He would have been dead within two hours — only having spent a few hours lost.

The difference between the two cases is dramatic, but demonstrates how important it is to keep your head and retain a positive mental attitude. The skier had panicked, and lost all mental ability. He had much better clothing, resources, and equipment and much more favorable weather conditions than the hunter. The hunter was able to compensate for his lack of equipment, however, by using his head and maintaining a positive mental attitude.

The Mechanics of Survival

Many individuals confuse a camping trip where you pack in all of your gear and "rough it" for a couple of days with an actual survival situation. If a person plans a "survival camping trip," if they are in control, and if they have some means to come out of the wilderness before they would perish, that person is not in what I define as a survival situation. What they are doing is practicing survival skills by testing their ability to adapt to various environmental challenges.

People who do this type of activity are developing skills and experience that make them much less likely to ever be in a real life-and-death situation, however. Practicing survival skills and the mental preparation these activities stimulate do contribute toward the positive mental attitude that is necessary to survive.

"Emergency" is a relative term. What is an inconvenience to one person may be a dire emergency to another. "Survival" is also relative to the individual but equally serious. You could put two people in an identical situation; one might consider it to be a life threatening event and the other might find it to be a walk in the park. The difference depends on the abilities, experience, and mental attitudes of the individuals.

THREE DIMENSIONAL THINKING

We have a tendency to be one dimensional and wasteful when we look at objects. We focus on the designed use of materials and block out other applications. Homeless people have nothing to live in and yet somehow survive difficult conditions for long periods of time. These people literally make one man's trash another man's treasure. They survive by living in boxes, old cars, culverts, and other improvised shelters.

As an experiment, look at the items in your trash can and see how many alternate uses you can come up with. Most people can see that a garbage bag could serve to carry water or other items, as a cover for keeping a pack dry, as a rain poncho, or as a waterproof layer on a shelter. But it can also be used to make a solar still to obtain clean water, as fuel to start a fire, or as a signaling device.

An empty pop can might be used to melt snow or gather and store water. Paper trash can make a ground cover for insulation, cover you as a blanket, or be used as fuel for a fire. A piece of cardboard can be folded and used as a splint, windbreak, shelter, or fire starter. A broken piece of glass can be used to fashion a knife, a scraper, or used as a reflector. A branch from a tree can be used as a tent stake, tent pole, crutch, splint and many other things. Several branches can be stacked and used as a shelter, for bedding, or fuel for a fire.

Make a game of coming up with alternate uses for these types of items. Talk to your friends and see if they can come up with other uses in a survival setting. Children are particularly good at this game. Starting to think in this way is your first step to becoming aware of how you would survive in an actual life-or-death situation. The second step is gaining knowledge of what is edible in the wild, of how to obtain safe drinking water, and of how to create shelter.

ASSESS YOUR PRIORITIES

If you find yourself in a survival situation, you first must determine what you will need to survive, which is dependent on the amount of time you will be in the dilemma. How long will you need to stretch your available resources? A person lost at sea might be facing days or weeks while a person stranded along a highway might be looking at only a few hours.

Modern search techniques, rescue training, and better transportation and navigational devices make it reasonably certain that any person who gets lost in the continental United States on land will be located within 72 hours after they have been reported missing. You must plan on using your available resources to survive for at least that amount of time.

Assuming you will be rescued within 72 hours you can determine the importance of each physical need. Water will be necessary. Even though it is possible to go longer than 72 hours without a drink, you can become dehydrated quickly and your condition will deteriorate.

Food will not become an issue unless you have a medical problem that requires eating regularly. Diabetics or those with hypoglycemia will be in serious trouble if they are unable to maintain balanced blood sugars.

Food and water, however, will not be relevant if you will die from exposure. Clothing and shelter may easily be your highest priority. Each of these survival necessities — food, water, clothing, and shelter — are discussed independently in this book. Each may take precedence over the others in a given situation, and each requires preparation, practice, and experience to efficiently fulfill.

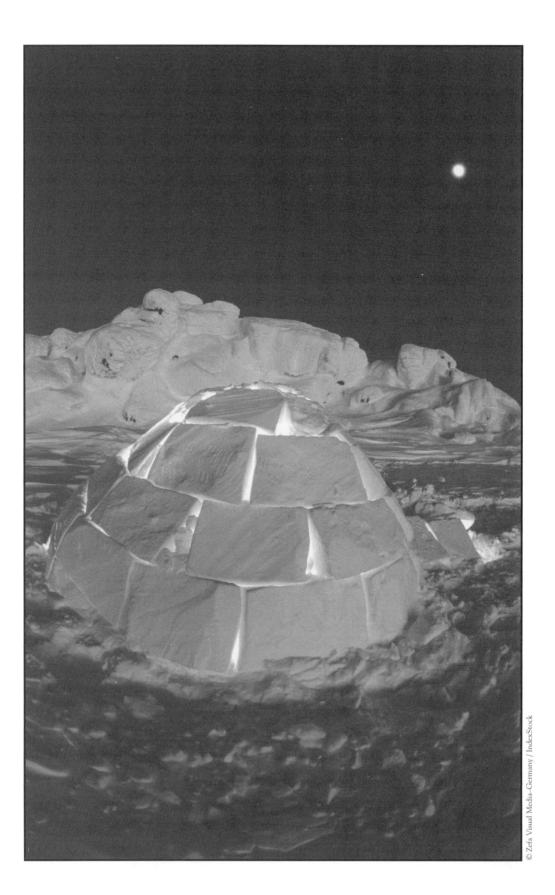

2
Shelter and Staying Warm

In the mid-1980s before cell phones were widely used, a doctor and his friend were snowmobiling in a restricted wilderness area (an illegal act) and got lost. The doctor had a cell phone, but it would only work from a high vantage point. The weather was getting very cold very fast and the doctor panicked to the point that he was willing and ready to pay any fines to get out of his situation.

Because of the elevation (and because of federal regulations regarding wilderness access) a helicopter rescue was out of the question. The helicopter we had available could not hover or land at that altitude but could only do a fly-over. We had a drop bag prepared for this type of call, which is a canvas duffel bag packed with sleeping bags, gear, dry clothes, fire starters, and other survival gear. The bag is designed to drop out of an aircraft to keep victims alive until ground teams can reach them. We had the helicopter drop the bag to the doctor and his friend.

The doctor was so afraid of losing cell phone contact that he stayed on the exact spot he got through to us, which was in the open, exposed to the wind and cold. We were getting very concerned that he would run the batteries down and finally convinced him to only call us every half hour on the half hour. Despite this he still never left the exposed location.

A ground team of very experienced snowmobilers were able to get to the stranded pair about three hours after the initial call. They found one snowmachine teetering on the edge of a cliff and the other machine severely stuck in the snow. The doctor was standing out in the open in the wind, and was very cold with his cell phone in hand.

The rescue team pulled the machines out, got them started, and took both men only a few hundred yards into the trees. Both men could not believe the difference the trees made, just getting out of the wind. The doctor's panic had taken over and blocked obvious solutions. The men were warmed up and brought back to base.

The doctor and his friend were cited and fined substantially for using motorized vehicles in a national wilderness area.

The Importance of Shelter

Many people we have rescued have decided to walk all night to stay warm. This is wrong, wrong, wrong. The heat you expend to stay warm by exercise depletes your body reserves at a very fast rate. You may feel better for the moment, but you are causing future problems. It is also difficult for rescuers to find you if you are constantly moving.

One of the most important and most often neglected needs is for shelter. Shelter is any means you can find that will protect you from your environment, and the environment determines how elaborate or how simple that shelter needs to be. In a hailstorm, you might just need to sit under a rock overhang or a tree branch, or you may need a windbreak, insulation, or some moisture barrier. In hot, open country, staying out of the sun may be your biggest concern, or in the snow, staying warm and dry.

Whatever your circumstances, you must be able to recognize a shelter or construct one out of whatever materials you have available. Homeless people are good at using minimum resources to make suitable shelters. A box, abandoned car, culvert, bridge, trash can — all will provide protection from the elements if you are resourceful enough.

Assess your situation and your environment. What threatens you now? What will threaten you when night comes or when the temperature drops? What changes can you expect? Be creative with all resources available. Plan for weather conditions to change and assume they will get worse.

Locate your shelter using a little common sense. If you build a fire under a tree that is loaded with snow, think about what will happen as the heat from the fire penetrates the branches. This might sound ridiculous but in case after case, I have talked to a lost person who struggled to get a fire going only to have it put out by a branch dropping its snow.

Additionally, select the location for your shelter where it can be seen by searchers. If you are hidden from view you are preventing those who are looking for you from finding you.

One example of a shelter that was not detectable was one in which a couple had dug a snow cave. Fresh and blowing snow had fallen during the night filling their tracks. Searchers on snowmobiles were following what tracks they could see. One searcher rode his machine over the roof of the snow cave, caving it in and not realizing what he had done. The couple was uninjured and located by the team when they turned back to search the area further. The rider only remembered hitting a soft spot in the snow.

Consider other needs and resources when selecting your spot. It would be foolish to build your shelter a long distance from your firewood or water supply if you could just as easily build it close by. Look around for potential hazards. Don't build a shelter in an avalanche deposition area. Don't camp under a dead tree that is ready to fall. Don't camp in areas that have a potential for flash flood or in a dry stream bed. The most important tool you can have when constructing a shelter is common sense.

Understanding Heat Transfer

When you determine the type of shelter you will need to construct, consider the four ways you will lose body heat: convection, radiation, evaporation, and conduction. Your shelter must protect you from heat loss in all four categories.

CONVECTION

Convection is heat being conveyed by air and air movement. Blowing on an object to cool it down is heat loss by convection. If you have gotten chilled because of standing in the wind, you have experienced heat transfer by convection. Stepping behind a windbreak may be all you need to stop this type of heat loss. Build a shelter that will place a barrier between you and the wind. Preventing heat loss by convection can be as easy as using a piece of plastic or cardboard to break the wind, or getting behind a tree, rock, or other object to stop the wind. An example of a person who did not deal well with this type of heat loss is the doctor and his friend from the story that started this chapter. If they would have simply moved out of the wind, they wouldn't have been so cold.

RADIATION

The body naturally radiates heat, and to prevent this type of heat loss we wear clothes for insulation. This is also the type of heat you feel when you sit next to a fire. Radiated heat will either be absorbed or reflected when it strikes an object. The more non-reflective the object, the more heat will be absorbed. Dark-colored, non-reflective clothing will absorb heat at a much greater rate than light-colored (more reflective) clothing in the same conditions.

When constructing a shelter you should use this type of heat to your advantage. A lean-to type of shelter could have a reflective back wall, such as a piece of mylar (the shiny space blanket) placed under the first layer of pine boughs. Then you can build a fire in front of the lean-to. The heat from the fire will be reflected off the wall and back onto the person lying inside the lean-to, similar to a giant toaster oven. If built correctly, a lean-to will reduce convection heat loss by breaking the wind, and offer heat by radiation. A large log or rock on the far side of the fire also helps reflect the radiated heat back toward the lean-to.

CONDUCTION

Conduction is when heat is transferred between objects when they come in direct contact. Heat migrates from the warmer object into the cooler one. In the winter, put your warm hand on a cold window. Soon the window starts to warm and your hand becomes cold. Likewise, if you sit on a cold rock, you will notice your behind getting really cold.

This type of heat loss is often overlooked when people are in a wilderness setting or building a shelter. A person will make a shelter that stops the rain, wind, and provides good insulation but then crawl in and lay on the cold ground and never warm up. What is happening is that the warmth in their body is being transferred into the cooler ground. The heat loss will never stop because the ground will continue to transfer the heat. You must separate yourself from the cold ground or all of your heat will be lost into the ground.

I have known individuals with top-of-the-line sleeping bags who could not get warm because they failed to insulate their bodies from the ground with a simple and inexpensive ground pad. The sleeping bag was working correctly, but they needed to have some sort of insulation to break the direct contact between their bodies and the ground.

Insulating your body from the ground can be done with any number of things including a ground pad, pile of leaves, pine boughs, cardboard, or any number of found materials. For years I used a silver-colored, bubble-wrap insulation that is sold in hardware stores for covering windows and air conditioners for the winter. It was only three-eighths of an inch thick and provided an excellent barrier under my sleeping bag. I rolled it up in the bag for transport, and it was extremely lightweight and inexpensive.

EVAPORATION

The body sweats to cool itself. If you're wearing a damp shirt in a breeze you will feel chilly even if the air temperature is hot. The moisture evaporating from the cloth causes a refrigeration effect.

Moisture can come from many sources and can be deadly. You can become wet from rain, snow, heavy dew, perspiration, condensation, walking in wet grasses, falling into a stream, or any number of ways. Your clothing and shelter must protect you from moisture. The shelter must be able to breathe to carry the moisture away from your body as it vaporizes. Nylon tents are very popular because the fabric sheds most water yet breathes enough to allow air to circulate and carry off the water vapors.

Plastic can be an excellent material to build an emergency shelter, a tent, a liner for the underside of a lean-to shelter, or many other things. However, you must make allowances for air circulation if you use plastics. If you put a warm moist body inside an airtight bag, the moisture your body sheds will condense on the plastic and eventually get you very wet. If air can circulate, it can carry the moisture away. To demonstrate this point, put on some plastic or rubber gloves for a while. When you pull your hands out, they will be wet and wrinkled as if you had soaked them in water, but it is only the moisture from your hands that has caused the wetness.

A sleeping bag wrapped in plastic will do the same thing. I once had the brilliant idea of keeping my feet dry in a sleeping bag by putting a large garbage bag over the bottom of the bag. The next morning I woke with a very dry bag except for the part in the garbage bag — my feet — and they were soaked with perspiration.

If you use plastic as a rain cover keep it several inches between you and the bag and keep the ends open so that air can blow through. Nylon tents use rain flies that mount over the top a couple of inches off the actual tent. The space allows water vapor from the warmer, lower tent to be carried away by moving air before it hits the colder upper rain fly.

Staying dry is necessary when you are constructing your shelter. If you are caught in wet or snow conditions, you might consider building a quick shelter to protect you immediately, then build a more elaborate, higher-quality shelter as conditions permit.

Selecting Your Shelter

Once you understand the types of heat loss and moisture problems, you can select and build your shelter to control those losses. Determine the type of shelter you can build based on your abilities, the environment, available resources, and the amount of energy you will need to expend to construct it. If you are totally exhausted, you will need adequate shelter with minimum effort. As you recover from your exhaustion, you can expand and improve your shelter as well as other comfort levels.

In looking for shelter, do not overlook the obvious; use common sense. If you are stranded with your vehicle, airplane or boat, you already have an excellent shelter. Think twice before deciding to leave that location.

NATURAL SHELTERS

Shelter can be as simple as getting under a fallen or standing tree, or crouching in a cave or under a rocky outcropping. Natural shelters might already be in use by wildlife so use caution, especially before entering a small cave or tangled mass of vegetation. Watch for animal signs such as tracks, discarded remnants of food, a worn path or freshly scratched earth near the entrance of a cave or den, signs that the cave may already be occupied. Enter carefully, especially during winter months when you may be waking something you might not be prepared for. Wild animals, even small ones, can be extremely dangerous if cornered in a confined area.

In hot summer months, snakes and other cold-blooded animals will enter holes and caves seeking relief from the heat. On cool but sunny fall or spring days, snakes will sunbathe on warm rocks.

LEARN SHELTER CONSTRUCTION FROM KIDS

Small children will often build little forts in the living room out of the coffee table, blankets, boxes, pillows, toys and other common items. They will crawl inside and have a little room all to themselves.

Children do not always understand the intended use of objects and will often use them in very strange ways. Kids build snow forts, tree houses, hideouts, caves and other makeshift shelters out of some of the weirdest things. They use all sorts of junk and end up with some cozy little shelters that are just big enough for themselves and maybe a friend.

This is the same resourceful thinking you need to build a shelter in the wilderness. You can pile branches, leaves, and pine boughs for a floor, insulating your body from the ground. You can stack sticks, logs, branches, and leaves to make walls and a ceiling. You can use branches, leaves, plastic, cardboard or other materials to make a blanket. Stack snowballs if that is what you have to work with and make yourself a snow fort or mini igloo.

Design your shelter to accommodate a fire and the smoke it produces. Place a fire in or near your shelter in such a way that your shelter won't catch fire or fill up with smoke, and as stated earlier, make sure no snow from above will fall and put out your fire once you have it burning.

Types of Shelters

LEAN-TO

A lean-to is a very simple structure. Its construction is as simple as the name implies — you lean something up against an object and use the protected area underneath as a shelter. The method of constructing the lean-to can vary considerably.

LEAN-TO

In a survival setting, a lean-to might be as simple as leaning stiff branches at an angle against a rock, trees or bushes and stacking pine boughs or other coverings on those branches. It could also be branches or logs leaned against a fallen tree. Placing a supporting log or branch between two trees and leaning smaller branches, trees, and brush or pine boughs against those supports is another construction method, and the one illustrated. Lean-tos are not complicated and can be built out of about anything.

There are some things you can do to make your lean-to more efficient, and many have already been discussed in the heat loss section. Placing a layer of reflective Mylar (the emergency space blanket you should have in your survival pack) as the first layer of the roof, before you start placing the branches and other items on top, will reflect body heat back toward the person lying underneath. The layer also makes the shelter rainproof.

A large log can be placed in front of the lean-to, or you can locate your lean-to just behind the log. The log will provide wind protection. Leave enough room between the front of your lean-to and the log so that you can build a fire pit. By having the fire between the lean-to and the log, the log will reflect heat back into the lean-to structure, reflecting off of the Mylar surface above. If you have a deep bed of coals in your fire pit it will radiate heat throughout the night.

Cover the ground with pine boughs or other insulation. Without some insulation barrier, your body will conduct heat into the ground, making you very cold.

While constructing the shelter, intertwine some of the smaller branches with each other. This will help tie the structure together in case you experience a gust of wind. Parachute cord or similar rope can be used to tie it together if you have it. Selecting a location that is somewhat protected will usually make this unnecessary.

I have spent many nights in many types of weather in lean-to type shelters. They can be thrown together very easily and can provide good protection. Often, they are easier than packing a small tent.

A-FRAME

An A-frame is very similar to a lean-to except that it has two covered sides with an open end. The construction techniques are also similar except that you'll need to find an adequate ridge pole for the sides of the A-frame

A-FRAME

to lean against. The ridge pole can be a large branch or a small tree that is about three to four inches in diameter and approximately eight to 12 feet long. Place one end of the pole into the ground and lean the other end into the crotch of a tree, between the crevices of two large boulders, on a stump, or other similar and secure structure. Then simply place branches, pine boughs, grasses, moss, etc. across the ridge pole to create the sides, leaving the large end open.

In mature forests, there are usually many fallen trees that make excellent ridge poles for both A-frames and lean-tos. Before you exert a lot of energy looking for the perfect materials, survey your surroundings to look for the obvious.

TREE WELL

A tree well or tree pit shelter is a good choice in snow environments. Find a tree with adequate lower branches to provide good overhead protection. Fir trees work the best. Break away the lowest branches and dig away the snow around the base of the tree. If possible, dig down until you hit the earth and then widen the pit until it is big enough for you and your equipment. Use broken boughs on the ground and against the sides for insulation. The tree above should offer a protective canopy, but if you need to stay for any length of time, you should erect a roof with branches and boughs.

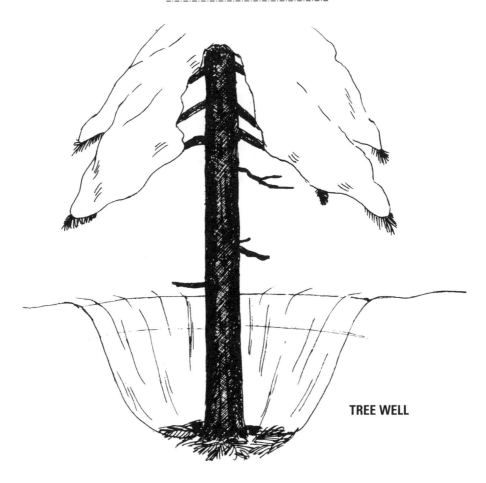

TREE WELL

Any shelter in snow conditions will get you wet in some manner or another. To keep the dampness under control, you should stop your project and dry out occasionally.

SNOW CAVES AND SNOW TRENCHES

Snow caves are very efficient shelters. They are not as easy to build as you might think and require a lot of practice to construct properly. I am not a big fan of the snow cave simply because of the amount of energy it takes to construct, how easy it is to get wet constructing one, and because of the lack of detectability. If you add heat such as a candle, you can also have a drip problem. With experience, you can learn how to handle these construction problems and how to glaze the interior to prevent drips.

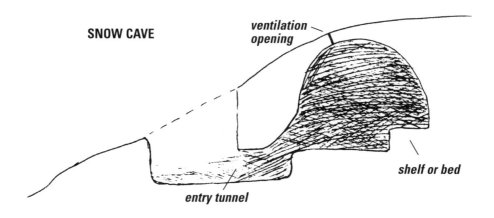

SNOW CAVE

ventilation opening

shelf or bed

entry tunnel

I have always preferred a snow trench type of shelter because of the simplicity and ease of construction. This shelter is just a trench dug in the snow with one end covered with branches and pine boughs. A nice fire can be built in the open end while you sit back in the covered area. The smoke escapes the open end while the heat radiates up under the covered end. Since the top is made with branches it does not drip on you. You can get more heat by placing space blankets on the snow walls behind you that will reflect heat back to your body.

The disadvantage of a snow trench versus a snow cave is that a snow trench is not as airtight as a snow cave, requiring a larger fire to stay warm which in turn requires more fuel. Gathering more fuel means expending more effort to maintain your fire. If you will be in your situation for any length of time, first construct a snow trench for immediate protection. Once you are rested and dry, spend your time and effort constructing a more efficient snow cave or other shelter.

If you plan to use a snow cave for shelter, you must carry a collapsible snow scoop or other means to dig the shelter. A ski, your hands or sticks can be used, but not very efficiently, and you will get very wet. Snow caves require an amount of snow that is deep enough for you to sit upright in, and large enough for you to lie down fully extended without touching the sides. Large snowdrifts are perfect because the snow is usually very firm and stable. The inside dimensions will be dome shaped with at least a four-foot ceiling and six-foot diameter. To have a four-foot minimum ceiling you will need one additional foot of snow for your ceiling. This means that a minimum sized snow cave will require five feet of snow depth.

This sounds like a lot of snow, but drifts this deep are very common and easily located. If you have less snow than this, consider a different type of shelter such as the snow trench, igloo or lean-to type of structure. An igloo can be made in the same manner that you built snow forts for snowball fights when you were a kid. If you have problems closing the top, put branches over it.

Start with the entrance of your snow cave, which will be two feet away from the six-foot diameter. This hole (from the surface down) will be large enough that you can easily get in and out of it. You must be able to bend over, scoop up snow and toss that snow out, meaning that the hole will probably need to be at least five feet in diameter. Since every situation is different, you may find a drift or other snow mass large enough that you can start digging horizontally immediately, without the need to dig down.

The floor level of your snow cave can be at any elevation in the snow, but digging down to the ground will provide a solid surface. Once you have gotten to the floor depth of the future cave, tunnel in under the snow bank. The entry tunnel will need to be about 24 inches in diameter, large enough for you to crawl in and out. Your tunnel should be at least two feet long before you start to dig out your room. The tunnel length is important because the tunnel prevents wind and other weather from blowing in. Without the tunnel, wind will blow in as if it is an open window.

Sitting outside of the tunnel, push your shovel in as far as possible and pull snow out to the entry hole. That same snow will have to be removed from the entry hole periodically throughout this process. The entry tunnel needs to be big enough to move snow through easily.

The floor of the entry tunnel will determine the floor level of your snow cave. Heat rises and the object of the snow cave is to create a dome-shaped structure that will trap heat. The entry of the snow cave is the only source of cold air in the completed structure, so if the entry is below the rest of the structure, warmer air will be trapped under the dome of the cave. In other words, everything you dig now will be higher in elevation than the snow cave entrance.

Continue to pull as much snow as possible from the outside until you have dug an area large enough to crawl into and continue digging. Once you are able to get under the snow, continue to dig and remove snow, tossing it through the entry tunnel into the entry hole. You will need to crawl out occasionally and clean the entry hole out so you do not plug up the entry tunnel.

You should construct a bed or shelf in the far side of the cave. This is easily done by compacting the loose snow. You can get rid of a lot of snow by compacting and shaping a bed (shelf) along half of the room.

Continue to dig and shape until you have created a domed ceiling about four feet high. Snow caves are much easier to dig in the daylight because you can watch the light as it passes through the snow and determine if you are getting too thin. You do not want to get so thin that snow falls through the ceiling.

Make your room as large or as small as you are comfortable with. Once your cave is completed and in use, you will not want to have contact with the walls, meaning that the room must be large enough for you to function without any physical contact with the walls. If you have a tendency toward claustrophobia, dig your shelter with the surface of the snow in mind. Remember that you can always bust through the ceiling to escape. Realizing this fact will often comfort people with this phobia to the point that they can relax and stay in the shelter. Even if your cave did collapse, you would be under a very light layer of snow, not buried as if you were in an avalanche.

Once the cave is dug to an adequate size, it is very important to smooth the interior of the cave. A rough surface with many little jagged peaks will begin to drip as the cave warms. Using the edge of your shovel and gloved hand, smooth the walls, especially the ceiling over your head, attempting to make the texture as smooth as possible. You are trying to accomplish a smooth glazed texture on the walls. Any drops of water that form will track down the wall to the sides of the cave, eventually creating a glazed interior surface that will make the cave even more efficient. The walls will be wet, so it is important that you and your gear stay away from these surfaces.

You also need to make a ventilation opening in the ceiling. This will help in slowing the condensation and melting inside the cave. The size of the hole will vary and need to be adjusted as conditions dictate. I will usually twist my shovel handle through the ceiling, making about a three-inch opening. A stick or ski pole will work just as easily. Three inches may be too large if you are near the surface or if you do not plan to use candles or other heat sources. If you cannot determine how large to make your ventilation hole, start small. You can always enlarge it later.

Once the cave is built, gather pine boughs, leaves, branches, etc. to use as insulation. Place these on the bed and lower walls to insulate you from direct contact with the snow and wet walls. If you have a good supply, cover the floor as well, which will help you stay clean and dry.

Next, dry out. The level of comfort you will have for your stay in the snow cave will be determined by how well you can dry yourself out. You have been working very hard, perspiring, getting wet from the snow, and you will be very damp. If you have a fire built outside, stoke it up and dry yourself thoroughly before climbing into the cave.

Once inside the cave, I recommend only a single candle for your heat source. Although the temperature in the cave will be only slightly higher than the freezing point, it will feel much warmer as you will not be exposed to wind, snow or other environmental chilling factors.

Practice digging a snow cave under controlled conditions. Experience will demonstrate the many problems that you will encounter. Many individuals enjoy winter camping and use snow caves as their shelters. The best method to learn snow cave construction is to see an actual cave. You can then experience the quiet, cozy and comfortable feeling they provide. Once in a snow cave, you will understand the need to maintain the inside temperature, comfortable, yet cold enough so as not to melt your shelter. You will also learn how to handle the moisture, heating, and ventilation problems the shelter will have.

3
Fire

We once tracked three snowmobilers who had been out overnight and were reported missing. Once the search was underway, it took only about 30 minutes to locate the three sets of tracks turning into very steep and difficult drainage, an area I knew they would not be able to ride out of.

Another rescuer and I followed the tracks on snowshoes. We did not dare ride machines down this drainage or we would be in the same situation. We snowshoed to the bottom of the drainage, traveling about a half mile and dropping very steeply in places. At the bottom we found the three snowmobiles, abandoned. The riders' tracks walked away, continuing to follow the drainage.

We called in by radio and advised the command post that we had a hot trail. We gave our location and began tracking the two men and a boy. A news helicopter was in the area, covering the search. We had progressed approximately a half mile from the snowmobiles when the news helicopter appeared overhead. They had been monitoring our radio traffic and wanted to get some footage and get involved in the rescue. As they hovered above us, the rotor wash created a blizzard from the snow in the trees and filled in the tracks we were following. We were not happy.

Fortunately we had already determined a direction of travel. The helicopter flew ahead and spotted the three missing persons. The helicopter could not land, but was able to direct another ground team to the victims' location to make the rescue. The missing people had camped about 500 yards from the highway but due to the terrain and trees, were unaware of it. They could hear traffic on the road, but were not sure which direction it was coming from or how far away it was. They had heard that sound travels a long way in the mountains and thought it was off in the distance. When they were found, they were heading down the drainage, parallel to the highway above.

The rescuer and I continued to follow the tracks because that was also the quickest route out to the road. We found an area where they had tried to start a fire. After we were also out of the woods, I met with the lost parties and learned that they only had a butane cigarette lighter with them and had struggled for over an hour to get a fire going.

They had spent the night under a very large spruce tree that was laden with snow. They had built their fire just outside the perimeter of the tree. Finally, they had a fire going, but the rising heat melted the snow in one of the branches and caused a load of snow to fall directly on their fire. They were unable to get it going again.

They could have easily started a fire with the fuels in the area if they had only learned a better fire-starting technique. For instance, spruce, cedars and other evergreens have very small dry branches that are out of the snow, protected by the larger branches. These little branches ignite easily. Evergreens also contain pitch that burns very hot, and even their green branches burn very easily. Not knowing these simple facts resulted in the group experiencing a miserable, cold night in the wilderness. It was simply luck, however, that the weather wasn't worse, nobody was injured, and we were hot on their trail. If the situation had been slightly different, their lack of fire-starting abilities could have resulted in a much worse outcome.

The ability to build a fire is one of the most important skills you must develop. The ability to quickly start a fire can make the difference between life and death. You must be able to start a fire in the worst weather conditions, when you are physically in the worst condition, or when your hands and body are so numb you can barely function.

Do you have trouble starting a fire in the fireplace at home or when you go camping? Are you the person who dumps a half-gallon of white gas on the wood or uses lighter fluid to get the fire going? Do you need three weeks worth of newspaper to get it going and then throw a big log on it and put it out? If you do, you will really have a problem getting a fire burning when it is wet, windy, or extremely cold.

Fire-starting is not difficult, but requires practice and preparation. You must know how and where to gather fuel that is dry and easily combustible even if everything else is wet. The term "building a fire" is exactly what you must learn to do. You start with the source of ignition, ignite kindling, and once that is burning, add larger fuels until you have a self-sustaining fire. Once the fire is going, you can use the heat to dry out additional fuels.

It is possible to rub sticks together and start a fire, but there are many easier ways. Review the techniques discussed in this chapter and practice them. Talk to others and see what they use to start fires. The sporting goods industry is always selling new gadgets and materials to start fires. Some are good and some are not. Experimentation is the only way you will determine what works for you.

If you need to start a fire, be resourceful. I do not recommend trying this, but on one search we found a man who, stranded on a snowmobile, was able to get a fire started by dipping a rag into his gas tank, then igniting it with an engine spark plug. This is a risky way to start a fire, but it probably saved his life.

Selecting Your Fire's Location

Use a little common sense in selecting a location for your fire. Place the fire where you will get the most out of it safely. Think about what will happen as the heat of the fire affects objects nearby. If you build your fire underneath a snow-laden branch, what will happen when the heat rises? (Although this sounds obvious, it happens all the time.) If you are in dry conditions, is it possible that you could accidentally start a grass or forest fire? If the wind direction changes, will you be in trouble?

Fire in snow is very safe. A fire can be very effectively built on top of the snow, but must be large enough not to go out as it melts down into the snow. I make a platform out of logs, then build the fire on top of that platform. By the time the heat gets into the snow, there are enough coals to keep the fire going.

In dry conditions, use a fire ring of rocks or dig a hole in the dirt to contain your fire. Be aware of dry or low-hanging branches that could ignite easily. Be aware of the sparks popping out of your fire circle and where they might land.

One fall I was doing a little primitive camping and had constructed a lean-to shelter. I built the shelter over an old bush and was using the bush to insulate me from the ground. I had a large log in front, about three feet away, to reflect the heat of the fire back into the shelter. I was not using any sleeping bag or blanket, just my clothing and the shelter to stay warm. I went to sleep that night quite comfortable. About three hours later I woke up very hot, and was impressed with how my system was working. Then I realized that the root system of the bush I was sleeping on was smoldering underground. The root system was burning, although the soil on top kept it from flaming up. It might sound like a good way to stay warm, but it took forever to extinguish that fire without digging tools or any large water containers.

In selecting your campsite or fire location, keep it reasonably close to your fuel source. If you run out of wood during the night, you won't want to go any distance to get more.

The Size of Your Fire

The bigger the fire the more fuel it takes to keep it going. In survival, we categorize fires as an "Indian fire" or a "white man's fire."

Indian Fire. An Indian fire is a very small personal fire, only six to eight inches in diameter. A person must constantly feed very small sticks to keep it going. A person who is comfortable in the backcountry will often use this type of fire if they sit for long periods of time.

Since this type of fire is very small, you will crouch over the fire and allow your body to absorb the heat. This type of fire uses very little fuel and does not put out much smoke. It is also not very detectable because you crowd the fire with your body.

This is a very efficient fire that is easy to maintain. The small fire does take constant attention because it does not build up a bed of coals and you cannot put wood of any size in it. This type of fire, however, is very good to use if you are mobile because it is quick to build, uses only very small sticks, and can be extinguished with your foot.

White Man's Fire. A white man's fire is the traditional campfire. This is the type of fire you build when you want to feel the heat from a distance. If you have plenty of firewood available, want to build a bed of coals so that

FIRE BUILT ON A PLATFORM OF LOGS.
This works very well in snow. By the time the fire gets to the snow, there are large enough coals to keep it going.

you can sleep for a few hours, or want lots of smoke or flame, then this is the style for you.

This type of fire will use lots of wood quickly. As a rule of thumb, you should collect as much firewood as you think it will take you to get through the night and then triple that amount. These fires form a very deep bed of coals that are easily restarted in the morning if the fire does go out. This larger fire is better if you need to dry out clothing or other gear.

Fire Starting

If you experiment with accelerants or other highly combustible materials, you must be extremely careful to avoid burning yourself or property. Any techniques should be practiced in a controlled setting before you go into a backcountry setting. Be aware of the combustibility of your clothing. Locate other flammables at a safe distance and never use these fire starting techniques indoors. You are responsible for your own safety.

You must plan for starting a fire. Every person who enters the backcountry should carry at least five different means to start a fire. Fire is such an important need that you must have backups on your backup systems. Carry a variety of systems to ensure that you can start a fire in any weather condition quickly.

BUTANE LIGHTERS

One of the most common and simplest fire starters is the butane lighter. This is a good overall lighter that is small, compact, and relatively simple to use. Its drawback is that it does not work well in extremely cold conditions because the gas does not easily vaporize. The lighter can be warmed up in an armpit or warm hands, if you have warmth left in your armpits or hands. The button and the flints on the lighter are small, making them very difficult to use when your hands are cold and numb. Also, butane lighters are dangerous if they happen to fall out of your shirt pocket and into the fire.

STEEL WOOL AND A BATTERY

Starting a fire in windy conditions can be very difficult. You must either protect your fire starters from the wind or use the wind to your advantage. One good source of ignition in the wind is using 0000 steel wool and shorting it across the contacts of a nine-volt battery.

Steel wool can be obtained in any hardware store, and is rated for coarseness with 0 being more course than 00, and 0000 rated as very fine. Once steel is ignited it burns very intensely. A nine-volt battery, the little square battery, works well because nine volts are hot, reliable, and the contacts are on the same end making them easy to use. They pack nicely and stay fresh in a film canister. The steel wool can be packed in a zip-lock freezer bag to keep dry.

Steel wool comes in pads that are a single layer wrapped up to make the pad. To use, unroll a strip of the steel wool and wrap it around another fire starter such as fire ribbon, magnesium, or other combustibles. Touch the battery contacts to the steel wool to ignite the fibers. You will see the steel wool start to spark and glow as it ignites and begins to burn. The windier or the more you blow on it, the more intensely it will burn. Magnesium, homemade concoctions, or other fire starters wrapped in the steel wool will ignite easily.

ROAD FLARES

My favorite fire starter in an emergency when you are cold, numb, wet, or otherwise in need of a fire immediately is a road flare. These are the fire sticks used by truckers, tow trucks, law enforcement, and others to provide a quick and intense light to mark traffic problems. They can be purchased at most auto parts or hardware stores and are very inexpensive. They usually come with a spike or nail sticking out of the base that is designed to jam into the ground. This spike should be cut off with a hacksaw, then dulled with a file so it doesn't put a hole in your pack.

Road flares are easy to handle, being about three quarters inch in diameter and about eight to twelve inches long. They light very easily by striking the cap over the end of the flare. They are designed for rough conditions and are somewhat moisture resistant.

Once lit, they will burn ten to fifteen minutes with a very intense flame. These work well in conditions where you need to start larger material rather than smaller kindling. The long burn time makes starting a durable self-sustaining fire easy. I carry two flames in my pack and reserve them for emergency fires.

MATCHES
Cardboard Matches. Cardboard matches work until they get damp by body moisture or other means. These matches will even absorb moisture from the air when humidity is high. They are probably the most inexpensive fire starter because convenience stores, bars, and gas stations are always giving them away. I always grab a handful when I see the bowl on the counter, not because they are great fire starters but just because they are free.

I have started many fires with matchbook matches, but usually end up lighting several matches or lighting the whole package at once to get them to work. They should not be a primary or secondary source of fire, but are better than nothing in an emergency.

Wooden Stick Matches. These used to be called "barn burner" matches when I was a kid because they were the ones kids liked to play with in the barn. These are the "strike anywhere" matches, and work much better than cardboard matches.

These matches are subject to moisture and will not flame up if they contain any dampness. They can be carried in a film canister to keep them dry, but you might have to cut them a little shorter to fit. I know many people who make their own waterproof matches by dipping wooden matches in candle wax to seal out moisture. This actually works well, but moisture can still be absorbed through the wooden stick. If you do waterproof them, keep then in a waterproof container.

Waterproof Matches. Waterproof matches are good in some situations but I have never cared for them because they do not provide a lasting hot flame and are easily extinguished in the wind. I do recommend waterproof matches as a backup fire-starting method.

MAGNESIUM FIRE STARTERS

Every survival catalog has the magnesium fire starter. To use it you are supposed to take your knife and make shavings from a magnesium block, hit that pile of shavings with a spark, and—presto!—you have a hot and intense fire. To further describe this method, in my opinion, "if bull—— were a snowflake this would be a blizzard."

This method of fire starting is about as primitive as rubbing two sticks together. Yes, it can be done, but there are easier ways. Try this in a controlled setting, then try it when your hands are so cold and numb you cannot grip a knife, let alone keep your shavings in a nice little pile, or keep that nice pile of shavings in your kindling. Then try to use that little flint that is even smaller than a knife.

I do recommend using magnesium as a fire starter because it does burn intensely and will resist moisture, but there is an easier way. My way requires some practice and preparation.

Talk to someone who finishes concrete for a living and ask them if they have an old magnesium hand float that they would give or sell. They usually discard them when the edges or handle wears out, but the float will still have a lot of magnesium in it.

In my shop I place the float in a vise and use a small block plane to make shavings. It is very easy to quickly make a lot of shavings. It doesn't really hurt the plane since the magnesium is much softer than the plane blade. I also use a rasp to make finer particles. I place these shavings and particles in a film canister for my pack.

In my pack, I also carry a welder's striker. This is the flint striker welders use to light a torch. They only cost a couple of dollars. Buy the inexpensive one that has a cup on the end around the flint.

To start a fire, organize your kindling and have other firewood available and ready to add. Hold the striker level so that the opening of the cup is facing up. Pour the magnesium into the little cup and strike the welder's striker. The magnesium will begin to burn. Work quickly and pour the magensium carefully into your kindling, in one spot, not scattering it around. You must work quickly, because the magnesium will burn hot enough to melt your striker.

Another method to ignite magnesium is with the steel wool and a battery as described earlier. Unroll the steel wool, pour the shavings into a single area in the wool, and then wrap it back up. Using the battery you can ignite the steel wool. This is an excellent method in windy conditions.

WELDER'S STRIKER

CALCIUM CARBIDE

One fire starter that works well in wet conditions is calcium carbide. This is actually a class three explosive that, when mixed with water, produces acetylene. It is often difficult to find. Talk to your high school science teacher for a source. Some hardware stores or welding suppliers will also have it available. Calcium carbide is used in carbide cannons and other noisemakers. Years ago it was used in miners' headlamps as fuel.

It is a granule that looks like black or dark gray gravel. When mixed with water, it begins a reaction that produces the acetylene gas. The more water added the faster the reaction will be and the more acetylene produced. Acetylene is a very combustible gas that only takes a single spark to ignite. The welder's striker mentioned earlier makes a good flint igniter for the flame.

This method is excellent in snowy conditions because you can place the carbide in the snow and hit it with a spark. As the snow melts, the water increases, and the more water the more acetylene, which equals more flame. You can then place your kindling over the burning snow and have a nice fire going quickly.

I carry the carbide in film canisters with the lids taped on to keep it dry. A film canister of the gravel type rocks is enough to start many fires. You will only need a few rocks to produce a nice flame. When you tape lids on to keep the contents dry, make sure you can still get the lids off when your hands are cold and numb.

FIRE RIBBON

Other items on the market that work well for getting an intense flame going quickly include fire ribbon, fire pastes, and fireplace log starters.

Look at the containers they come in to make sure they are durable enough for your pack. You do not want to carry a paste or liquid in a package that is easily broken or punctured, as it will be all over in your pack.

HOMEMADE CONCOCTIONS

Gunpowder and Fingernail Polish Remover. A homemade concoction of 3841 rifle gunpowder mixed with fingernail polish remover makes a good fire starter. Gunpowder is made up of many small granules that are varnished to keep them separated. The fingernail polish remover dissolves the varnish making the granules stick together.

Using a plastic bowl and wooden popsicle stick (to reduce any chance of spark), put the gun powder in the bowl and stir in enough fingernail polish remover to make a sticky goo. Once it is of a sticky consistency, use the popsicle stick to pack the goo into a film canister. Work neatly. If you slop the goo all over the place or get it all over yourself you will be in trouble if it ignites. Once the fingernail polish remover is added, the rifle powder becomes much more stable.

There is a big difference between "black powder" and "rifle powder." Black powder flashes explosively when ignited but rifle powder is a much slower burning powder, and consequently much safer to work with. Use a plastic container with a wooden stick to stir to reduce any chance of spark. Experimenting with gunpowder can be dangerous, so use your head. No smoking of course, and this is not for children.

The gunpowder/fingernail polish remover concoction is used in its wet, sticky form. The amount in a film canister, once ignited, will burn like a giant match head for three to four minutes. If it dries out (and it will eventually dry out), it will shrink and become a very hard rock. It will still work as a firestarter, but it will burn much more intensely and burn out much quicker. It will not be explosive

A good igniter for this method is steel wool and a battery. Take the goo out of the film canister, wrap it with steel wool, and touch the steel wool to a nine-volt battery. The steel wool will ignite the powder quickly.

SAWDUST AND KEROSENE

Sawdust soaked in kerosene, diesel fuel, or lantern oil can be kept in a plastic film canister. Chainsaw sawdust works the best because it is a larger chip, but any sawdust will work. Soak the sawdust in the diesel fuel, then pack it tightly in a plastic film canister. To use, place the contents in a pile on your kindling and ignite. Do not scatter it around. The pile will produce a much more durable flame. It can easily be ignited with a match, lighter, steel wool and battery, or similar.

CANDLES

Candles make excellent fire starters. Use the candles that are about one inch in diameter and about one inch tall. These small candles have many uses, including light in a tent or car. I shave the candles down so that they fit tightly in a plastic film canister for my pack. The film canister helps keep candle wax from getting all over the pack.

One method of fire starting using a candle in rainy or windy conditions is with a plastic bag. Place your kindling and other fuels inside the plastic bag. Hold the bag in a position to block the wind and rain and light the candle down inside the bag. The candle will have a much more durable flame than either matches or a lighter. The plastic bag protects the fire until the fire is large enough to consume the bag.

FLINT AND STEEL (THE PRIMITIVE METHOD)

Using flint and steel is one of the most primitive methods to start a fire. They are difficult to use when wet but can easily be dried out and made useable again. The steel is a rough file-like piece of steel and the flint is a very hard rock or actual flint rock. Striking the rock against the steel generates a few sparks. This primitive method includes using a fabric carbon patch that will begin smoldering with only a single spark from the flint. The carbon patch is ignited, then wrapped around a kindling such as dry grasses or very dry and very thin wood shavings. The smoldering carbon patch is then blown into a flame. That flame is then built into a larger fire.

The fabric carbon patch can be made by cutting two-inch-square patches of 100 percent cotton cloth. Make sure it is 100 percent cotton, no synthetics. Put the square patches into a metal tin box, such as some candies or cough drops come in. These are the little tins that are about two inches by three inches and about one-half inch thick. Place the patches in the box and close it. I like to wire it shut so it doesn't come open, then put the box in a camp fire. You then burn the cloth without any oxygen getting into the tin. A properly-cooked fabric carbon patch will still be

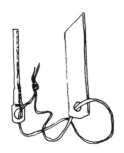

METAL MATCH
Supposed to make fire starting easier, but the small parts are difficult to handle. There are more reliable methods.

black burned fabric that is somewhat flexible and will stay together. If you cook it too long or too hot, it will be burned to a brittle patch that will crumble when handled. The only way you will be able to learn this technique is to practice, practice, practice. The temperature of the fire and length of time will be different in every case, but 15 to 30 minutes in the fire should produce useable carbon patches.

This is a very difficult technique to master because you must learn how to strike the flint to get a spark. You must be able to make the spark hit the cloth. You must be able to make a fabric carbon patch properly. You must be able to obtain the extremely dry and flammable kindling that can easily be blown into a flame, and finally be able to build that flame into a durable fire.

FLINT AND STEEL (THE EASIER METHOD)

The primitive flint and steel method takes experience and lots of practice to be a reliable fire-starting technique. Flint strikers that are used by welders are much easier to use. They can get wet or damp, but can easily be dried and made usable again. The welder's striker can be purchased at any hardware store. They are designed for use with bulky welding gloves and will work well with your winter gloves on or when your hands are cold and numb.

The welder's striker has a cup on the end that can accommodate magnesium, sawdust with diesel fuel, dry kindling, carbon patches, or other similar fire starting materials. Hold the striker level and place the material in the cup, careful not to interfere with the flint or striker surface. Hold the striker against an object to steady it and ignite. Once the material is burning you can place it in your kindling.

MAGNIFYING GLASS

A convex-shaped piece of glass, such as that from a magnifying glass, binoculars, a broken bottle, or eye glasses (in a pinch) can be used to ignite tinder by focusing the sun's rays into a concentrated ray of heat. The tinder will first start smoking and then glow red. Blow gently onto the tinder to encourage a flame.

PRACTICE, AND BRING BACKUP SYSTEMS

There are many ways to start a fire, and many tools, tricks and techniques are available. Talk to people who do a lot of camping or other back country activities and see what they use. Practice the different methods and see what works for you in all the various conditions. Carry at least five different methods of fire starting since this ability could make the difference between life and death. Test your systems and ability in the worst weather conditions and see if you can really do it.

Carry at least five different methods of fire starting, since this ability could make the difference between life and death.

As training on a cold day, take off your gloves and let your hands become as absolutely cold as you can stand it and then try to make a fire. You will experience problems that you may not have thought about before — the little lighter buttons cannot be depressed, the butane won't light, matches cannot be held or will not stay lit, and many other problems. Practice your technique in a controlled setting, not when your life depends on it. You must have the ability to start a fire 100 percent of the time in the worst weather conditions.

Fire-Starting in Wet Conditions

It is easy to get caught in heavy rain, snow, heavy dew or other wet conditions when you are out in the wilderness. The ability to start a fire in wet conditions can make the difference between life and death, since these conditions are much more dangerous.

Experience and preparation will be invaluable in your fire-starting ability. If you are planning a trip into the wilderness, waterproof your pack. Place your fire starters in containers that will keep them dry even if you get moisture inside your pack. Keep the fire starters inside different packages so that if one is violated you will still have dry supplies. Ziploc bags, film canisters, and other similar plastic containers work well to keep firestarters dry.

Practice different systems and see what provides the most reliable ignition. Some systems work well for some individuals, but are difficult for others. You will not know what works best for you without practice.

FINDING DRY FUEL

"Everything is soaked, what will I burn?" Even though everything appears wet you can still find dry kindling if you know where to look. Use common sense and look for areas that are naturally sheltered such as under rock overhangs or under logs.

If there is downed timber or branches turn them over and look for dry material. Larger logs will often be elevated off the ground, which keeps them dry. They may have a rotten core that is up and out of the weather. I look for old rotten logs and will dig out some of the "punk wood," the old, dried out, rotten core of the log. If insects have been eating in it, it will have areas of paper thin wood that will light easily. Look for dry areas in the rotten log.

Standing dead trees have plenty of dry fuel. If the bark is loose, you can peel chunks of bark off and then peel kindling off of the protected underside. Dead tree branches in standing or living trees make good kindling. Trees absorb moisture from the root system, not through the bark. Even though the bark looks wet, the wood inside will be dead and dry.

To tell if branches are dead and dry, try breaking them. If they are dead and dry they will be brittle and snap cleanly and easily. If they are at all flexible they are green and will be difficult to ignite.

In the wintertime, when trees are dormant, they will all look dead. Do the snap test on little branches, looking for ones that are about one-eighth inch in diameter to start your fire, and add larger wood as the fire takes off. Living cedars and evergreens have many dead and brittle branches in the tree if you look closely. Evergreens and cedars also have a natural pitch that burns very hot when ignited. Once you have a few small branches ignited, you can add some of the living green branches.

Evergreens and dead trees usually can be spotted from a good distance. When selecting a location for your campsite, look for one near a good fuel source.

Fire-Starting in Windy Conditions

Starting a fire in windy conditions can be just as frustrating as starting one in wet conditions. Matches and lighters blow out, as can the fire once you get it going. You have two choices when starting a fire in the wind: either block the wind from your fire until you get it started, or use the wind to your advantage.

The method of starting a fire with a candle in a garbage bag (discussed earlier) works very well because it blocks the wind until you have a good fire started. Get behind any object that blocks the wind or use your body as a windbreak. Windbreaks can be as simple as getting behind a rock or tree or digging a hole down in the snow. It is also wise to find a location out of the wind because you need protection for yourself.

The steel wool and battery method is excellent in windy conditions because the wind intensifies the burn of the steel. Use this ignition method to light other fire starters, such as magnesium, that also become very intense in the wind.

Road flares produce a durable flame that can withstand tremendous wind. I have never seen a flare blown out from the wind alone. The flare burns down inside a tube and will become more intense in the wind.

4

Water and Food

Water

The ability to obtain safe drinking water is one of the most important skills you must develop. When you become dehydrated your body loses the ability to circulate heat effectively making hypothermia more likely. Dehydration also diminishes a person's mental abilities, which are of utmost importance when in a survival situation

When people get into trouble, it is a human tendency to focus on the big problems and ignore a little problem like thirst until it becomes so intense it becomes a big problem. When a person is in severe dehydration, the desperation for water becomes so controlling that a person will eat or drink just about anything for moisture, ignoring any health risks.

If you become lost or are hurt in a remote area, plan for water early. Consider the need for water a top priority before that need becomes desperate. Maintaining your body fluids is wiser than becoming dehydrated and trying to recover those fluids. Anytime you feel you might need to shift into a "survival mode," start to make mental notes of ponds, streams, or other water sources or clues of water in the area.

Avoid any and all alcohol. Alcohol stimulates the need to urinate, which dehydrates you further. Alcohol is also a depressant, and you need to stay positive. If you are dehydrated already, alcohol will intoxicate you more quickly than normal because your body is trying to find fluids to replace the loss. The ratio of blood/alcohol will be much higher than is normal with the same amount of spirits, which is not what you want when you need to keep your head clear. If you have some type of distilled spirits, use it as a fire starter but do not drink it.

Water from an unknown source can be very dangerous. Water often contains substances that can cause more problems than going without a drink. Giardia, parasites, chemicals, airborne pollutants, animal feces, poisons, dead animals and other pollutants are very common in water. Parasites and other pollutants can cause diarrhea, taking more water out your body than it can absorb. Knowing the source along with how to purify that water is the only way you will be able to safely get a drink.

WATER FROM SNOW

Snow is ice. If you are already cold, putting ice into your body will make it colder. Eating snow will contribute to hypothermia or can at least start you in that direction. Hypothermia (which is discussed later) is a life-threatening problem.

Snow is also not necessarily clean. Fresh snow is relatively safe but old snow is subject to dirt and other pollutants that land on it as it ages. Snow forms in layers with each storm adding another layer. Each layer is exposed to the elements for a period of time and accumulates pollutants. As the snow melts, the water settles and carries pollutants down through the layers below. Additionally, there are parasites that thrive in snow, such as "snow fleas." This snow is usually recognized by a pinkish tint; I will assume you already know not to eat yellow snow. Despite all of this, snow is still a good source of water in a survival situation.

Water often contains substances that can cause more problems than going without a drink.

Look for clean, white, fresh snow to melt for drinking water. If you have ever tried melting snow for water, you soon realize that it takes a whole lot of snow to make just a little bit of water. Melting snow will also require advance preparation, packing something along for you to melt the snow in. You cannot efficiently melt snow over a fire in a plastic cup so carry a non-insulated metal cup. Fill your plastic water bottle with the heated water and use it under your clothes as a hot water bottle.

Snow can be melted using a plastic water bottle too. When you choose your water bottle select one that has a wide mouth, as it is much easier to pack snow in the larger opening. Fill the bottle with snow and put it between your layers of clothing (not directly against the skin). As you walk, build a fire, etc., your body heat will start to melt the snow. When the snow starts to melt, shake the bottle to help the water melt the remaining snow. When you drink water out of the bottle, refill it with snow and shake it again, allowing the remaining water to melt the snow. Do not drink your bottle below one half full and you will have enough water left to continue the process. This method is much safer than eating the snow directly because you can control the cooling effect on your body.

If you must melt snow in a plastic water bottle near a fire, do so very carefully. Use an *ungloved* hand and hold the bottle near the fire, close enough to be warm but not so hot as to melt the bottle. Holding the bottle in an ungloved hand allows you to monitor the heat.

TIPS FOR FINDING WATER SOURCES

Finding water in non-snow conditions requires practice and experience. Following a drainage downhill will often lead to some source of water. Do not forget the obvious if you are in areas with livestock. Look for windmills, water tanks, or whatever livestock may use for a water source. If you have a dog along, let it run loose and follow. When a dog gets thirsty, it will sniff out water and go to the source. Also notice game trails. Wild animals need water and will have a favorite watering area. The traffic patterns might give some indication of a watering hole. A good rule to follow is that if two game trails come together and form one, the single trail will be the one that might lead to water. Multiple animal droppings are a sign water is near. Additionally, don't forget to watch the birds. Birds usually fly toward water in the early morning or just before nightfall. Flocks of waterfowl will also circle over water during the day.

FINDING WATER BY VEGETATION IN OPEN AREAS

When scouting larger areas, pay attention to the vegetation. Cattails and plants with dense leaves or bright green color give a hint of possible water. Color is one of the best clues because bright green, lush, or heavy vegetation needs lots of water. If you notice an area that has vegetation different than everything surrounding it, it may be worth checking out. Trees also thrive near water sources. A string of trees winding through a valley floor usually indicates a stream. While hiking in different areas, practice locating water sources. Try this in different terrains and see how successful you would be if your life depended on it.

Interestingly, earthen dam inspectors use vegetation as a means of finding water. They observe the vegetation and look for any changes from previous inspections. If an area has more color or lusher growth, it could indicate that water is seeping through.

SPRING WATER

Untreated spring water should only be used if you know the source and how pure that source is. What appears to be a spring is often just surface water that has gone underground, traveled for a distance, and then resurfaced. Actual springs may contain dangerous chemicals or other pollutants. Natural, pure spring water that is safe for drinking is becoming increasingly rare. Unless you know for a fact that a particular spring is safe, you should not drink the water without treating it first.

OPEN WATER: STREAMS, CREEKS, PONDS AND RIVERS

Water is purified naturally as it passes over rocks and is aerated and exposed to ultraviolet sunlight. Open water, streams, and rivers cannot be considered safe to drink, however, because they are exposed to animal waste, man-made pollutants, and other natural pollutants. *You cannot determine the purity of water by its clarity.* Clear water may look more appealing but can contain bacteria, parasites, or chemical pollution not visible to the naked eye. Likewise, cloudy water does not mean that it is not safe to drink if treated. Water is cloudy because of aeration or particulates that are in suspension. These particulates are not necessarily dangerous.

I was four-wheeling with a friend in the San Juan Mountains in southwestern Colorado a few years ago. We were coming down a mountain pass on a remote four-wheel drive road and came across a sheepherder's camp that had about five hundred head of sheep. A mountain stream was running through the middle of this meadow. The floor of the camp was a solid mass of sheep that covered the stream for hundreds of yards.

We continued on our trip through the camp, following the road down along the stream for about another half mile. At this point if you looked back up the road, you could not see that there were any sheep farther up the road.

Another jeep with three occupants had come up the trail from the opposite direction and stopped at the stream. The three occupants had their faces in the stream and were sucking up "pure rock mountain water."

We stopped and visited with them and listened with interest to their comments of how "there is nothing better than clean, pure, mountain stream water."

Not only do animals defecate in water, they also die in it. It is not uncommon to find a rotting carcass lying in a stream. I do not recommend drinking from a stream without some means of purification.

Purification Methods

Since a natural source of pure safe water is difficult to find, you need to be able to make the water you do find safe. There are many systems, gadgets, and purification chemicals on the market that can help you do that. The different systems all have advantages and disadvantages; some are costly and some use chemicals that can cause medical problems.

BOILING

Boiling water is one of the safest methods to treat water. Water must be boiled for long enough to kill all of the impurities, which is at least 10 minutes. This is difficult in a backcountry setting because you normally do not have pots that can hold much water. Try boiling water in a metal cup and see how much water you have left after 10 minutes.

Since boiling a reasonable amount of water is difficult, it should be considered as a secondary method of water treatment when planning your survival pack. If you do have the means to boil water, save your other treatment systems for when boiling is not practical.

Practice boiling water (seriously). Build a campfire and use the metal cup or other containers that you would normally have in your pack. Maintain the boil for ten minutes and experience the problems. This will help you to determine what equipment you will need when planning a trip.

IODINE PILLS

Iodine pills work well for the most part. The pills must be in the water for some period of time before they are effective, so if you are thirsty, you must patiently wait. Two to three drops (or pills) of iodine to every two pints of water need to be left to stand for 30 minutes. Iodine pills work best in clear water, not in water containing a lot of particulates.

I personally do not like the taste the pills leave in the water, especially when using them for several days. I have tried using Tang and other flavorings to mask the taste, but have only ended up with funny-tasting Tang.

When using iodine pills, or any chemical treatment, you must be careful to clean the rim of the container thoroughly before you take a drink. Typically a person will dip a water bottle in a stream to fill it, put the pills in the water, put the lid on the bottle and allow the pills to work. Untreated water can be trapped on the rim of the bottle in the threads under the cap. When you take the lid off to drink, you should rinse the rim with some of the treated water to be safe.

Individuals with thyroid problems may have a problem with the iodine. If you have a question regarding whether you should use this type of chemical, consult your doctor.

The advantages of iodine pills are that they are very inexpensive, compact, and relatively effective. A very small bottle of pills will treat a lot of water. I recommend iodine pills as a back-up system, but not as a primary water purification system.

WATER FILTERING SYSTEMS

There are several filtering systems that work very will. When selecting a filter, make sure that it filters the water down to at least two microns. The lower the number of microns it will filter, the cleaner the water will be. For example, a two-micron filter will not filter out a one-micron particle. The higher the number the bigger the particles that pass through will be. However, the smaller the filter the faster it will plug and need replacement, and the smaller the filter, the more time and effort will be needed to push water through.

Some filters combine filtering with iodine or other chemical treatment, as filtering alone does not purify water.

Straw Filters. The straw type of water filter works very effectively for a quick drink. They are good in backpacks because they are very small — usually about one half inch in diameter, six inches long, and only an ounce or two in weight. The disadvantage to the filter straw is that you either need to put your face in the water source or use a cup to pick up the water. The straws can also require some effort to suck water through, especially if they are beginning to get plugged from use. Additionally, if you are in cold weather and the straw has water in it from previous use, it will freeze up in your pack. Lastly, the straws only filter as you drink, so you are unable to filter water for other purposes.

Regardless of these drawbacks, water straws in a survival pack are highly recommended. I recommend carrying two, and packing them in different parts of your pack just in case one is damaged. They are relatively inexpensive and can be used as a primary water treatment system.

Water Filtering Pumps. I use a pump-type ceramic filter. It pumps water from the source by a hose into your container ready to drink. These can be expensive, ranging in price from fifty to several hundred dollars. A quality pump is very durable and will last many years. If you determine the cost by the number of gallons each type will purify, a quality pump is cheaper to operate in the long run.

The pump I use is about one and a half inches in diameter, six inches long and weighs about a pound. The hose on the pump is about three feet long allowing you to reach the water away from the bank, which is usually cleaner. It is also easier to get water without getting wet.

When selecting a filter, look at how well it is built. Some of the inexpensive models have plastic parts that are easily broken. A quality filter should have metal nipples where the hoses attach and can take considerable abuse.

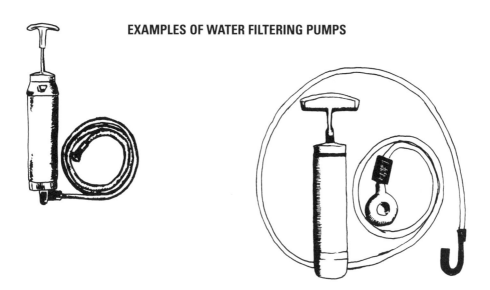

EXAMPLES OF WATER FILTERING PUMPS

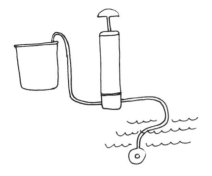

USE OF A PUMP FILTER

Ceramic filters can be easily cleaned and will last much longer before you need to purchase replacement filters. I highly recommend a high-quality ceramic type filter that has metal or high strength features as your primary water treatment system.

For a trip into the backcountry or elsewhere where you will use a full-size backpack, I recommend carrying a non-insulated metal cup, a large mouth plastic water bottle, one straw filter, one bottle of iodine tablets, and one quality ceramic-type water pump filter.

In a survival pack, your small day pack, or fanny pack, you should carry at least two straw filters, iodine tablets, a large mouth water bottle, and one non-insulated metal cup.

This might seem like a lot of equipment to pack, but water is one of the most important necessities of survival.

Solar Stills

In a dry environment you may need to obtain your water with a solar still, which captures the moisture that is contained in the ground. Using a solar still is a slow process that does not produce much water, so you may need several stills to fulfill your needs. Hopefully you will have the materials available to build a few of them. The water you catch will be distilled and safe to drink provided your plastic and containers are clean.

The basic principle of a solar still is simple. You dig a hole that is then covered with plastic. The moisture within the hole will condense on the underside of the plastic and drip into a catch basin ready to drink. This sounds easy but it must be done correctly to work.

Inventory your resources and see what you have available for plastic. Garbage bags, a space blanket, or any other sheet plastic will work. If you have a large sheet of plastic you may want to cut it up into smaller pieces, since many smaller stills will work better than a large one.

You also need some sort of catch basin for each solar still. This could be a pan, an empty tuna can, the bottom of a pop can, a hubcap from a

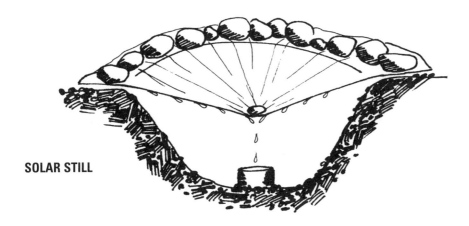

SOLAR STILL

vehicle, a styrofoam cup, or any number of things. If nothing else is available, you can dig a small hole within the larger hole and line the smaller hole with plastic, making sure it does not leak.

First, dig a hole that is much smaller in size than the plastic you will be using to cover the hole. You will need to *completely* cover the hole with the plastic and have enough overlap to seal the edges. The hole must be deep enough so that when you place a weight (such as a rock) on the plastic directly over your catch basin, no part of the earth touches the plastic on the inside of the hole. Placing green vegetation such as grass, or anything else that contains moisture in the hole under the plastic will greatly improve the still's performance. Again, the hole must be deep enough so that nothing placed inside touches the plastic.

Once the hole is dug, place your catch basin firmly in the center of the hole. Add green grass, leaves, etc. to the sides of the hole. Next, drape the plastic over the hole and secure it around the rim with rocks, dirt, or sticks. To make the water drip into your catch basin, place a small rock or some small weight directly over the basin. The plastic should now have a single low point directly over the catch basin that is several inches lower than the outside edges. The smaller the catch basin the more accurate your low point must be. Once the solar still is ready, seal the edges of the plastic with loose dirt so that no air can escape from the hole.

If you have transparent plastic, you will soon see water droplets condensing on the underside of the plastic. As the water droplets get larger they will start tracking down the plastic to the low point under the little weight and drip off into your catch basin. It will take some time to get a significant amount of water.

MAKING YOUR SOLAR STILL MORE EFFICIENT

Every time you remove the plastic to check your water supply you will lose the water droplets that are forming on the plastic and allow the moist air to escape. If you are creative and have something you can use as a straw, place it in your catch basin during construction. This way you can suck water out of the catch basin without interrupting the process. Normal, everyday straws can be extended by telescoping them together, or a small rubber surgical hose will work. If you use any hose off of a vehicle make sure you know what you are doing. Many hoses on a vehicle are used on systems that are very poisonous.

If you are using a styrofoam cup, a pop can, or anything else that will easily tip over, dig it into the ground or fill around it with loose dirt. You do not want your catch basin to spill after all that work.

ADDING MOISTURE TO THE STILL

There are many things that contain moisture in addition to green vegetation that can be added to a solar still to increase the moisture content. Since the water is distilled, the process will purify it. Urine can even be added because the distillation process will purify it, but be careful not to over spray into the catch basin.

Never use antifreeze, window wash fluids, or any other automotive fluids in your solar still to add moisture! These fluids contain deadly forms of alcohol that will evaporate and condense at the same rate as water. They will condense and appear clear just like the water but they will still be deadly poisons. Even trace amounts of antifreeze can be deadly. Do not use hoses from your engine's cooling system for anything you will consume. A vacuum hose is the only hose I would consider using because they normally just move air. Even these hoses can contain some old gas and oil, so you must know what you're doing and be careful.

BE RESOURCEFUL

It would be unlikely to have everything you need to put a solar still together. If the only thing you have is a piece of plastic, such as a garbage bag, you will be able to get the job done. Space blankets might work but the reflective coating will keep them from working very well.

To dig a hole you will need a shovel. If you don't have one use your hands, a stick, a screwdriver, a tire iron, a pipe, sharp rocks, a board, or anything else to loosen the ground. The hubcap on a vehicle can be use for a shovel in a pinch.

Locate your still directly in the brightest sunlight. It is the warmth of the sun hitting the bottom of the hole and the vegetation that causes the moisture to evaporate. The warmer the hole gets, the faster the process.

WATER CONSERVATION

If you can find no water, try to conserve what water is left in your body. Limit your physical activity during the day. Walk or do other strenuous physical activity either early in the morning or at dusk. Avoid sweating by walking or working at an easy pace. Also, do not eat unless you have water to drink with the food.

Food

Food is rarely an issue in a wilderness survival situation. Humans can survive long periods of time without food, some longer than others. However, individuals with diabetes, ulcers, or other medical conditions could quickly be in trouble as a result of not eating. If you are one of these people and you are venturing into the wilderness, you must carry enough food in your pack to sustain you for a minimum of 72 hours.

People with medical conditions that require balancing blood sugars (diabetes) will need foods that contain sugars and carbohydrates. Most foods obtained in a survival setting will consist mostly of animal protein. Some fruits, nuts, and berries do have a high sugar and carbohydrate content, but odds are they will not be in season when you are lost.

You may be fortunate and find berries, nuts, mushrooms, or other treats but be aware that many wild plants can be dangerous. Unless someone who knows the native plants has taught you, it is usually safer to go without food. Some plants in the wild look exactly like something that grows in your garden. Do not assume they are safe. There are plants that have beans and pea pods that appear just like the garden variety but are very poisonous. To be 100 percent safe, do not eat any wild plant with a bean or pea-like appearance.

Many wild plants cause hallucinations, sickness, and/or diarrhea. Diarrhea might only be an inconvenience at home but it can be life threatening in a survival situation because of the rapid dehydration it can cause. Below is a chart with other wild plants to avoid.

Plants to avoid

- *mushrooms (some are edible, but unless you are 100 percent certain, don't eat one)*
- *umbrella-shaped flower clusters (do not even try the Universal Edibility Test with these plants, as their sap will often cause blisters if it contacts the skin)*
- *plants with a milky or black sap*
- *bulbs*
- *carrot-like leaves, roots, or tubers*
- *bean or pea-like appearance*
- *shiny leaves or those with fine hairs*
- *white, yellow, and green berries*

INEDIBLE PLANTS *Avoid plants that look like these if you have any doubt at all about what they are or whether they're edible.*

There are a few edible wild plants that can be easily identified by most people, and that grow throughout the United States and Canada. These are shown in the illustration on the opposite page. If you are unsure of a

EDIBLE PLANTS *(left to right): cattail, dandelion, grass, pine. All parts are edible.*

Edible Foods

- *grass: stems, roots, and leaves are edible; don't eat black or purple grass leaves*
- *cattails: in spring, the young shoots and flowerheads are the most edible portions and can be peeled and eaten raw or boiled. During summer, the flower's pollen can be eaten raw.*
- *pine trees: sharp needles arranged in bundles of 2, 3, or 5. Pine needles may be eaten raw or cooked. Boiled in water they make tea. The layer between the bark and inner wood can be eaten raw or cooked. The seeds, located under the scales of the cones, may be eaten raw or cooked.*
- *common green seaweed: seaweed on shore is probably rotten; instead, gather it off rocks or directly from the sea.*
- *dandelions: the entire plant is edible; leaves and buds are the best.*
- *chickweed: grows throughout North America; the leaves are dandelion-like; flowers are light blue. The leaves and roots are edible.*
- *crabapple: small, tart fruit can be eaten raw or boiled.*
- *water cress: a surface water plant that thrives wild throughout much of the county; sometimes seen abounding in a luxuriant green mat overflowing a shallow trough at the edge of a slow-running stream.*
- *purple, blue and black berries are usually edible.*

plant's identity or if you are unsure if it is safe to eat, there is a process called the **Universal Edibility Test for Plants** (this test does not apply to mushrooms and fungi). I repeat, however, that it is safest simply not to eat when you are in the wild unless you absolutely must.

Universal Edibility Test for Plants

Separate the plant into parts: leaves, roots, stem, flowers, buds. Test only one part of the plant at a time and in one preparation method. Do not ingest anything other than treated water during the test's duration. Fast for 8 hours before beginning the test.

First, choose a small amount of one portion of the plant (i.e. the leaves), and break them/rub them on the inside of your wrist or elbow. If you experience any burning, rash, or other irritation, stop the test; do not ingest the plant. If you experience no symptoms, take the portion of the plant and prepare it the way you want to eat it (raw, fried or boiled are the most common). First place a small portion of the prepared plant on the outside of your lips. If no burning, itching or irritation occurs after five minutes, then you can proceed to place the plant on your tongue without chewing. Wait an additional 15 minutes. If there is still no reaction, thoroughly chew the plant without swallowing, and wait 15 more minutes. If there is no irritation or numbing sensation, swallow the plant.

Once you've swallowed the plant, wait an additional 8 hours and watch for illness (nausea, vomiting, diarrhea, cramps). If you experience ill effects, induce vomiting and drink plenty of water. If after 8 hours you have experienced no sickness, prepare a half cup of the plant the same way as before and consume. Wait an additional 8 hours and if you still feel well, the plant is safe to eat when prepared in that manner.

Do not assume that the plant is safe to eat prepared in any other manner (i.e. if tested cooked, do not assume you can eat it raw, and vice versa). Also, one part of the plant may be edible and other parts inedible. You must test each part of the plant before you can assume it is safe to consume. Different people may respond differently to the plant as well.

Never eat any dead animal you might find, no matter how good its condition appears. I have talked to many individuals who think a deer, rabbit, or other animal that is frozen in the snow is still okay to eat. First, you do not know how or why that animal died. It could have been diseased or poisoned, perhaps a problem that could be passed on to you. And if you have ever stayed in a snow cave you know that the temperature under the snow is a constant 20-30 degrees no matter how cold it is outside. This is not cold enough to safely preserve frozen meat for any period of time.

If you have the means to hunt or capture an animal and butcher the meat yourself, you will have an excellent source of food. Thoroughly cook any meat from wild animals that you plan to eat in order to kill any parasites or bacteria. Squirrels, birds, turtles, frogs, snakes, grubs, worms, insects, fish, or anything that crawls, walks, waddles, swims, or flies on its own is a good source of food.

For small game, you may be able to throw a fist-sized rock to stun or kill a rabbit or squirrel. Although this is not easy, you can improve your odds by tying the rock to a rope or stick, which is then easier to throw and aim. Precise aiming takes practice and energy, and is required to be successful at killing a quick-moving, darting animal. Aim for the animal's head or shoulder region, and practice your throwing skills before you are in a survival situation.

Never eat any dead animal you might find, no matter how good its condition appears to be. You can't know why it died.

If you have a knife, you can whittle a stick into a spear for killing fish. It is easiest to spear fish in shallow streams, although this is also not easy and requires practice. You can use small twigs or a safety pin in place of a fish hook, insects for bait, and anything that will work for the line (a long stick, thread, rope). Avoid eating fish that has a bad odor, is slimy, or if its flesh stays indented after being pressed.

EDIBLE BUGS:
Grasshoppers, snails, grubs, and earthworms.

Perhaps the easiest things to eat in the wild but perhaps the least palatable to most people are insects. Edible insects include grasshoppers, ants, snails, grubs, and earthworms. All can be eaten raw or cooked. Remove the spiny legs of grasshoppers before you eat them, as they can get lodged in the throat. Avoid insects with bright colors and those that carry parasites such as flies, mosquitoes, ticks, centipedes, and spiders.

INSECTS TO AVOID *(left to right): Caterpillars, spiders, ticks.*

The need for food must be dealt with early if you are in a dire situation. Food must be gathered while you still have the mental and physical strength to do so. If you wait until the hunger is intense and the situation desperate, you might not have the strength or mental ability to make sound decisions. Patience and calm nerves are definite requirements when trying to kill an animal or catch a fish with "found" materials, and intense hunger will lessen both. If you suspect you will need to survive for more than 72 hours, start planning for food immediately when your strength is at its peak.

Ration your energy. If you waste more energy attempting to obtain food than it will provide, you have not accomplished anything, and made matters worse. Although less appealing, the physical effort to capture insects and other crawly things will be much less than trying to hunt and capture larger animals.

Recommended Food for Your Pack

If you are planning a hiking or camping trip, there are many foods that are lightweight and still offer good energy. Power bars or candy bars are lightweight and do not require any preparation. Experiment with different brands as some will create thirst or leave a bad taste in your mouth.

Dehydrated meals have become very popular and work well for backpacking. They do not spoil, can be quite tasty, and weigh very little. Some of these meals can be somewhat bulky and expensive, however. Prepare sample meals in the backyard or at a camp. Some dehydrated meals are lightweight and compact but might require pots, pans or other containers to prepare.

One meal I have found to work well that is lightweight and inexpensive is made with Soupstarters. These are dehydrated vegetables with broth and flavors added. They can be carried in the original container or put in plastic sandwich bags. To make a meal, use a non-insulated metal cup, boil a little water, add a little Soupstarter and some jerky, let it stand for a while, and you will have a nice hot stew. Many other "add water and cook" meals could work equally well. Experiment in a controlled setting.

Jerky and other salty foods are also good but will create thirst. Plastic bags of trailmix work very well; they are easy to pack, do not spoil, and do not require any field preparation.

5

Wilderness First Aid

In 1978, I was coming home from a job about 60 miles from home. The project was in a very rural area, near one of the Indian reservations in South Dakota. I had been married for only a couple of years, struggling financially, and working at whatever jobs I could get. I was also a hunter, and at the time, coyotes were bringing $70-$80 per pelt. This was a lot of money, if you could bag a coyote. It was mid-February and the pelts were in prime season.

One evening I was driving home and spotted a coyote sitting just alongside the road. It is illegal to shoot from the roadway, but there was no traffic, and I was not a real fanatic about some of the game laws at the time. I had my coyote rifle, a Mini-14, with a 30-round clip ready to go. As my pickup stopped, the coyote took off running. By the time I stopped the truck and got off a round, the coyote was over 400 yards out. I let off a couple of rapid rounds and made a fantastic shot, rolling him at a dead run.

The coyote was injured but not yet dead so I took my automatic .22-caliber pistol out to finish him off. I fired a round into the coyote, killing him, then shoved the gun into the holster I was holding in my hand. The tip of my glove caught the trigger and I fired a round at point-blank range through my leg.

The bullet entered the very top of my leg, near my hip. It happened so fast that I did not realize what had happened. The first thing that hurt was my knee; the blast had snapped my knee backward so fast that it caused pain in the joint. I was standing there, now realizing what I had done, and it was -20°F. I was not in pain, although somewhat stunned by my stupidity, but I knew it would be hurting soon. I was alone, a quarter mile from my vehicle, and knew I better be getting back while I still could.

I never thought to look at the injury. I could have shot the femoral artery, the sciatic nerve that controls my leg, or had other serious injuries. I was wearing insulated coveralls and other winter clothes and never checked the wound. I walked back to the truck, and by the time I got to the fence line, my leg was "really talking to me." I drove myself to the nearest town 10 miles away. Once in town, I asked a woman to drive me to the hospital, which she did, 15 miles away.

At the hospital the doctor told me how lucky I was. The bullet did not exit; it was about an inch from going clear through. It passed only a fraction of an inch from the artery and nerve, and had hit the bone but not damaged it. There was a spot of blood about the size of a dime around the entry wound. I recovered fully, except for my pride.

I could have bled to death or been permanently crippled. Unable to walk, I could have frozen to death. I had no idea what to do or how serious the injuries were. This made me realize how dramatically things can change in a moment.

About one year later, I was employed on a construction project in Yankton, South Dakota. It was a multi-story building, and at the time only the superstructure was up. One night after work, about 5:30 PM, most of the crews had left the job site. A few of us were into archery and had set up a little archery range on the ground level, under the building. The only people left on the job were a few framers, working overtime, on the upper floor. It was after normal working hours and all the offices, phones and other communications were locked down in gang boxes.

All of a sudden a strong gust of wind blew through the building. It had been calm and this was a surprisingly strong gust of wind. We decided to quit the archery if the wind was going to blow, and go home, when from around the building a man came running up, shouting for us to call an ambulance; someone had gone off the top. We didn't understand him and the phones were locked down so I chased him to find out what had happened. By then I was outside the building and he yelled back, "A man on a scaffold on the top floor went over the edge." The man had been working on a scaffold 15 feet away from the edge of the building. The gust of wind had tipped his scaffolding over, pitching him over the edge of the building.

70

I turned to go back and tell the others, but when I turned around, I was looking at the man lying in front of me. He had fallen 85 feet. His body had struck the crossbars in a section of scaffolding and then busted through a single scaffold plank, landing in a pile of brick rubble. The bar and plank had broken his fall. He was still alive.

The man searching for help had by this time run to an office across the street to call 911. I was left with this seriously injured person, not knowing what to do. All I could think to do was to keep him still until help arrived. This seriously injured man was starting to regain consciousness, starting to move around, starting to talk. The ambulance and EMTs arrived moments later.

I had no idea how seriously this man was injured. In doing their assessment, the EMT gently lifted the man's scalp. His hair lifted off like a bad toupee; his skull had broken open like a watermelon dropped on the floor. We were looking right into his head at his brain, yet the man was alive and starting to talk. He was packaged, loaded and transported to the hospital nearby.

I had no idea what to do or how serious the injuries were. This made me realize how dramatically things can change in a moment.

I called the hospital later that night to check on him and was told by the staff he was doing very well; he would survive. I was shocked. I had expected to hear that he would be dead, or at least permanently disabled. The nurse continued to state, in fact, that the manner in which his head had broken open probably saved his life. The open skull allowed his brain to swell without additional injury.

The man recovered and visited the job site about six months later. He was not 100 percent at that time, but was expected to recover fully. This incident made me think about first aid, although I didn't act on it at the time. I did not have any idea what to do or how to act — he would have died if it had been up to me. My performance bothered my conscience.

About one year later my family and I had moved to the Denver area. I was driving back from a camping trip in the mountains with my wife. We were many miles from Denver, yet the traffic was very heavy along the single lane highway. The traffic had come to a crawl — obviously something had happened up ahead, such as an accident, stalled vehicle, construction, we could not see. The line of traffic was backing up for several miles. Literally hundreds of cars were in line, creeping forward. Finally, we approached the problem, a severe car accident.

The accident had just happened and no emergency personnel or police were yet on the scene. A jeep was pulling a trailer, much too large for the vehicle, and its driver had lost control. The trailer had flipped the jeep, ejecting and seriously injuring the two occupants. The trailer then detached from the vehicle, impacting a Volkswagen van head on. The van was carrying a family and their condition was not good. The driver, who appeared to be the father, had been decapitated; the other passenger in the front seat looked like the mother, and she was not alive. It was obvious that at least three others in the back of the van were seriously injured. In all there were two fatalities and five very seriously injured individuals. There were hundreds of cars backed up, and hundreds of people had rolled past the accident. Only one man had stopped and was trying to render aid to these five survivors. He was obviously overwhelmed.

I reacted like every other irresponsible person, demonstrating my morbid curiosity, gawking, just like everyone else. I didn't know what to do. I was no better then anyone else that passed by. I justified my actions for the moment, in my mind: "I would only be getting in the way;" "This was someone else's responsibility;" "I don't need to get involved;" "I need to get home, I don't have time for this."

This scene stuck in my mind and bothered me for many years. How could I have driven by and left that one man to handle all those victims. How cold I must be to abandon those children who had just lost their parents, thinking, "This is someone else's responsibility, someone else's problem." I visualized the headless body, the dead mother, wondered how the kids made out. I could see the injured bodies lying in the road, the man running frantically back and forth, from body to body, doing what he could.

In the early 1980s, I moved to Steamboat Springs. To get a hunting license it is required to take a hunter safety course. During the course we were shown a film about Search and Rescue. I was interested in doing something like that and asked the instructor about it. He advised me to contact the local Sheriff's Office. I did it the next day, and they called in the acting President of Group. I only expressed an interest, no commitments or application. He took my name and phone number. The next day, I was pulling up to the house when my wife came out stating, "Search and Rescue is on the phone. They have a lost person and need you to come down." That was my first mission and I was hooked.

I was entering into the world of EMS. One of my first courses was Basic First Aid; I would not abandon a desperate emergency scene again.

Knowing What Action to Take

The wilderness setting creates a totally different environment when it comes to first-aid. Most emergencies will be very serious, the result of traumatic injury, cardiac emergency, skeletal injury, bleeding, hypothermia, anaphylactic reaction to food or insects, or a serious medical illness. The only sure thing is that the emergencies seem to always happen in the most rugged, most inaccessible locations you can possibly imagine.

The first-aid decisions you make must be dictated by two things: (1) What action will give the injured person the best possible chance of survival? (2) Do no harm! Do not cause additional injury or unnecessary pain and suffering by exceeding your own capabilities.

Reading a chapter in a survival book will not qualify any person to make sound first-aid decisions. First-aid training must be obtained through an accredited course, taught by a qualified instructor in a classroom setting, one in which practical skills can be taught and tested. Every emergency is unique and may require many difficult decisions by those involved. The best course of action in one emergency may not be the best in another. In order to make good decisions, you must have the information, education and experience that only first-aid training can provide. You must have this education before the emergency arises. Every person, as a minimum, should have CPR and basic first-aid training. The time invested is well spent.

In a truly life-threatening situation, any action is better than no action! If the person is going to die anyway, you can't hurt him or her by trying something, anything — just take some action. Bad CPR is better than no CPR. If CPR is needed, the patient is finished without it; attempting CPR, at least, offers the possibility of hope.

Death is a fact of life. People die as a result of accidents and illness and sometimes there is nothing anyone can do about it. The tragedy is when a simple maneuver or simple action could have saved that life, and it was not performed. This can be as simple as opening an airway.

The following is an actual case of a 911 call. This call demonstrates how knowing a simple maneuver can save a life. A woman called 911 to report that her husband was unconscious. She had found him in bed, not breathing, but making a gurgling noise and near death. The dispatcher was EMD (Emergency Medical Dispatch) certified and began to assess the situation over the phone. He asked the woman what position her husband was in and she stated he was lying down in bed, with a pillow behind his head. The dispatcher advised the wife to remove the pillow from behind his head, letting his head rest flat. Once his head was flat with his body, he immediately started breathing, and soon regained consciousness.

The man had passed out due to another medical problem and while in the relaxed state, his airway was closed only because of the position of his head. Since he was not able to breath, he did not regain consciousness. The simple act of removing the pillow from behind his head saved his life.

Had the wife had minimum first aid training she would have recognized the problem immediately, since both CPR and basic first-aid training teach two methods of opening an airway. The "Head Tilt," which just tilts the head back to open the airway (used here), and the "Jaw Thrust," pulling the jaw forward, used when there is a possibility of neck or head injury or anytime it is undesirable to move the neck. It would have been a tragedy if the man had died because someone failed to perform such a simple act.

KNOWING WHEN YOU CAN'T HELP

Consider a wilderness scenario in which you are hiking with a friend, he clutches his chest and falls face-down, unconscious. What do you do? Do you run for help, leaving him alone? Do you stay and provide CPR? Where do you go for help? How long will it take you to get help? Which action offers that person the best possible chance of survival: leaving to activate EMS or staying on the scene to give CPR?

This is a very difficult situation. Without a pulse, the person will be dead within minutes. Without a professional response, the person has a very low chance of survival. You will only be able to perform CPR for a limited amount of time before you will be exhausted. Any attempt to move the patient will cause additional strain to an already strained cardiac system and would probably prove fatal. You will not be able to perform CPR while moving the victim, so if he has not regained a pulse, he will be dead. It is also almost impossible to transport an unconscious person without assistance or some equipment.

Sometimes there is no right or wrong action, when nothing you could possibly do would save the other person. But once you have taken the time to obtain first-aid training, you can take comfort in knowing that you did all that could have been done. A person without any training might blame himself for not knowing what to do.

WHAT WILL YOU DO IF AN ACCIDENT HAPPENS?

One effective method of preparation and training is to put yourself in scenarios mentally, then determine what you would do in each case. Pre-plan and review, in your mind, what actions would work and what actions would cause harm. The more thought you give the situation, the more you realize what needs to be done.

My basic first-aid classes were taught at a local mountain college that used the same classroom as the EMT classes. I happened to find an EMT instruction manual in the room that was full of gory pictures — severed limbs, gunshots, burns, and other very gruesome scenes. These were like the things I had already seen, and I started to think about how I would deal with those situations if faced with them again. The pictures were not minor injuries; they were crushing injuries, fatal, disfiguring, disgusting images that really stuck in your mind. As I thought about it, I realized these are actual injuries, real people, real lives, and not some special effect for a movie. These were people, just like me, with families, friends, and real lives. Having seen what I had, and then seeing those pictures, I had a good idea of what a real scene would be like when I had to deal with it.

Test yourself: place yourself in the following scenario and think about how you would respond. Be honest.

It is a dark night, the hour is late and you are alone. You are traveling and become tired, pulling off a distance along a remote road for a little nap. Out of the darkness a person covered in blood from head to toe, possibly having very disfiguring facial injures, staggers toward your car. No one in the area knows you. Would you be afraid, reacting as if it were a zombie from a sci-fi movie? Would you just leave, pretending that you didn't see anything, either out of fear or not wanting to get involved? Would you realize that this is a seriously injured person desperately needing help?

Many people would leave the scene, out of fear or desperation because they don't know what to do. Many would be afraid of getting involved. Some would leave and call the authorities anonymously.

But what if this was a helpless woman, having just escaped a ruthless rapist? What if this were a victim of a plane crash, having used his last ounce of strength to seek help? What if you were the only realistic chance of survival that person had, and you just drove away?

Using scenarios really works. Reviewing the scenes in the manuals and my own previous experiences, made me think about how I would handle emergencies in the future. I thought about how I must learn to manage my composure and render aid.

Within two weeks of completing my first-aid class, I was involved in a very serious accident on a construction site. I was able to put what I had learned and what I had planned to the test.

I was a supervisor for a mechanical contractor on a large commercial project. The owner of the general contracting company was visiting the job site. I had some business to discuss with him. I saw him walking through and started heading in that direction to catch up and talk to him.

Over his head, about 20 feet up, a laborer was stripping concrete forms next to a very large, steel I-beam. It was 40 feet long and 24 inches deep—a very heavy piece of steel. It was not attached to the building, but sitting in place for the next concrete pour that would tie it into the building.

The owner stepped through a doorway, just out of my sight, and then came flying backward out of the door, landing on his back. The I-beam had fallen, striking him on his hardhat, knocking him backward and rolling down his body.

The hard hat saved his life, glancing the beam off and throwing him backwards, but it had come down on his leg, chopping it off, about mid-calf. He didn't realize what had hit him. He was conscious, groaning, "Oh my leg, oh my leg."

I approached him, as I had just been trained to do, and assessed his injuries quickly. He was conscious, but spurting blood from the stump where his leg had been. Less then one half inch of skin was holding the lower part of his leg to his body.

Two other supervisors on the job were nearby. One panicked and ran for help while the other applied pressure to his femoral artery. I applied pressure directly above the injury, controlling the bleeding. The severe bleeding stopped within seconds; we had saved his life. The fire department with paramedics on duty was right across the street and responded within only a few minutes.

Having prepared mentally for the incident made me able to deal with such a gruesome scene. Not shocked by the blood or by the injury, I was able to do what needed to be done. The scenes I had reviewed in the book helped me to prepare.

The ambulance sped off toward Denver, 100 miles away. A "flight for life" helicopter responded to rendezvous at mid-point. At the hospital, the owner's leg was successfully reattached. I saw him walking about six months later, limping, but making a good recovery. It felt good to know that I had a part in keeping that man alive, and that I had a part in his ability to walk. Unlike the earlier accidents in which I did not help, I had a good conscience this time.

It was my conscience that forced me into emergency services; I could not leave an injured person again. I learned what I must do to help. Likewise, you must learn what to do to help.

Get First-Aid Training

I cannot stress enough the need to seek and obtain first-aid training before the need arises. Accidents happen when they are least expected; it could be someone very close to you. The training you receive could be called upon anywhere, not only in wilderness survival situations.

Although I will discuss each of these first-aid techniques, you need to get face-to-face training on how to control bleeding, how to recognize and treat for shock, how to treat injured limbs, how to immobilize various areas of the body, how to deal with impaling injuries, and how to recognize and treat heat exhaustion, hypothermia, and other common emergencies. In no way does the information in this book replace a first-aid course.

In the wilderness, environmental factors such as terrain and weather, along with the severity of the injury, make the appropriate action different in each case. The ability to adapt to the uniqueness of each situation is the basis for wilderness first aid. I will provide common scenarios and common problems, based on actual emergencies that demonstrate the unique problems that are encountered in the wilderness, and what you might be able to do to overcome those problems.

Wilderness first aid will take much more action on the part of the injured person's companions than normal. Making decisions as to what action to take requires education, experience, and some common sense.

Basic first aid in the wilderness will often require improvising equipment. Be creative, look around at your resources and try to be three-dimensional in your thinking. Throughout this chapter, I've included some suggestions for helping an injured person with available materials.

Assessing the Injury

If someone with you is injured, you must act immediately. The manner in which you handle your patient will be determined by the injury and the way the injury happened. The way an injury is caused is called mechanism of injury. For example, if a person falls 20 feet and breaks their leg, the obvious injury is the broken leg and the mechanism of injury is the fall. If a person stepped in a hole and broke their leg, and had the same broken bone, the injury would be treated differently based on the mechanism of injury (the hole).

A broken leg from stepping in a hole is simple because there is no threat of head, neck or back injuries, and no potential for internal injuries. A broken leg from a 20-foot fall has many potential injuries that might go undetected. Landing on your feet sends the impact up through the entire body — hips can be broken, the pelvis fractured, the spine compressed or fractured, or the neck damaged. The jarring of the internal organs can cause serious damage. A broken leg might be painful enough to mask the pain of other injuries, or the brain could have been jolted enough to mask symptoms and pain.

Never underestimate how badly a person is injured by the obvious injuries. Many people have walked away from car accidents thinking they were fine, only to return to the hospital with other complications.

Artificial Respiration

If a person is not breathing but has a pulse, you must restore breathing immediately or he or she will die in a short time. Make sure the patient is on a resonably firm surface and clear the airway of any blockages. First, tilt the patient's head back and place the heel of your hand on their forehead, raising the chin. Pinch the patient's nose with the thumb and forefinger of the hand that is resting on their forehead. Take a deep breath, place your mouth tightly over the victim's mouth, and blow air from your mouth into their mouth. Stop blowing when the patient's chest is expanded. Watch for the patient's chest to fall. Keep blowing breaths into the patient's lungs at a rate of 12 breaths per minute until the patient begins to breathe on his or her own.

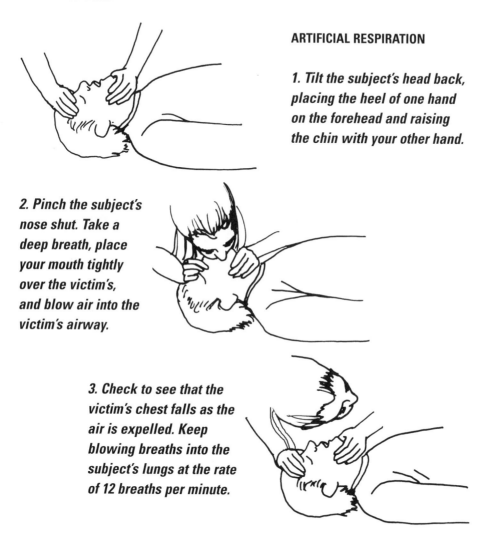

ARTIFICIAL RESPIRATION

1. Tilt the subject's head back, placing the heel of one hand on the forehead and raising the chin with your other hand.

2. Pinch the subject's nose shut. Take a deep breath, place your mouth tightly over the victim's, and blow air into the victim's airway.

3. Check to see that the victim's chest falls as the air is expelled. Keep blowing breaths into the subject's lungs at the rate of 12 breaths per minute.

Cardio-Pulmonary Resuscitation (CPR)

CPR is used when a person has stopped breathing and has no pulse. It should only be performed by someone who has had training in the method, so again, I stress the need for you to take an emergency first-aid training course. Do not perform this technique if there is even a slight pulse. Chest compressions carry the risk of further injury from broken ribs, so don't perform CPR unless you are certain it's needed.

Basically, CPR is a combination of chest compressions to get the heart beating again, and artificial respiration to get the lungs working. You should give 60 chest compressions per minute with a breath and a slight pause after every five compressions. CPR is easiest when there are two people to help, one to perform the chest compressions and the other the mouth-to-mouth respiration.

Bleeding

Most bleeding is controlled by direct pressure on the wound with sterile gauze. I do not carry sterile gauze in my survival pack. If a person is bleeding badly, I am not worried about infection as much as I am his bleeding to death. You need to stop the immediate life-threatening bleeding and get him to a hospital where they can prescribe antibiotics for the infection. If by some chance you have hydrogen peroxide or a bottle of distilled spirits with you, then by all means clean the wound. But otherwise, concentrate on stopping the bleeding.

Some of the things that make good bandages are cotton fabrics: tee shirts, underwear, socks, bandannas, or similar clothing. Depending on how and where the injury is located, you might be able to tear the garment in strips or tie it around the injury with enough pressure to control the bleeding. Direct Pressure simply means applying pressure directly to the wound for at least five minutes. Do not delay in applying pressure even if you don't have a bandage to do so (use your hand if that is all you have). If the wound is on an arm or leg, elevate it above the heart level.

A belt works well to apply direct pressure on a wound. Although it may be difficult to tighten enough to shut down circulation deep within a limb, it can be wrapped and tightened enough to apply good pressure on the wound and dressing.

Once any dressing is applied, do not remove it to check on it. The bleeding stops because of the clotting of the blood with the fabric. The seal from the dressing holding the wound closed also prevents infection and additional bleeding. If you pull the dressing off just to check it out, you will reopen the wound and start the whole process over.

If you have applied dressings to a wound and it continues to bleed, do not remove the original dressing. Continue to apply additional dressings over the original covering, stacking one on the next. It is common for the original dressing to slow the bleeding considerably; removal of this bandage will only destroy any progress you have achieved.

Once you have wrapped a wound, make sure there is still adequate circulation below the wrapped area. For instance, if you've wrapped a knee, feel for a pulse in the ankle. If you can't feel a pulse, your bandage is too tightly wrapped.

PRESSURE POINTS

Applying pressure to an artery between the heart and the wound will decrease the amount of blood flow from the wound, but this method is not always effective. You must apply pressure on the pressure point for at least 7 to 10 minutes for it to work. In general, pressure points are at your joints (see diagram), but to learn precisely where the pressure points are, you must be trained.

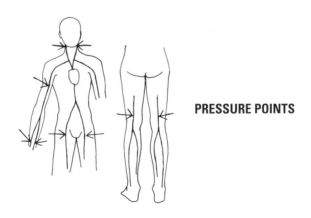

PRESSURE POINTS

TOURNIQUETS

A tourniquet is never used except as a last resort. The decision to use a tourniquet is simple: should you sacrifice the limb to save the life? Proper application of a tourniquet is taught in first-aid classes. A tourniquet can be made out of a bandanna or similar cloth using a stick as a means to tighten it firmly. A belt can be used, but it is difficult to tie tight and then maintain that tension. The stiffness of the leather also causes more damage to the muscle than a cloth band. Once you have applied a tourniquet, it should never be loosened.

To apply a tourniquet:
1. Apply a three to four-inch cloth several inches above the wound.
2. Wrap the cloth around the limb several times and tie it into a square knot. Place a sturdy stick in the middle of the knot.
3. Turn the stick to tighten the tourniquet until the blood flow stops.
4. Secure the stick in place with additional cloth. Note the time when the tourniquet was applied and seek professional medical assistance immediately.

Immobilization

In order to "Do No Harm" it is usually necessary to immobilize the person or parts of the person and transport him or her as quickly as possible to an ambulance or other medical facility. Any traumatic injury will warrant some sort of immobilization.

SPLINTING

Splinting can require a little creativity. The rule for splinting is that, at a minimum, it must immobilize the break plus one joint above the injury and all joints below. For example, if a person has broken their ankle, you must immobilize the ankle plus the knee above and the entire foot below. If the upper leg is broken, you will be immobilizing the entire leg, the hip and pelvis, and possibly the entire lower back.

If a bone is sticking out of the skin, do not try to push it back in. Do try to clean the wound and cover the bone end with a wet cloth (to keep the bone from drying out). Then apply the splint, securing the wet dressing in place. Remember that when you are wrapping the splint, check for a pulse below the injury to ensure that adequate circulation is continuing through the extremity.

The proper manner to immobilize is taught in a first aid class, but many times you must improvise a splint. Be creative. Many materials will work. The splint must be rigid to provide support for the injured part. It should also be comfortable, avoiding pressure points, and protect the injury from the environment.

Do not limit your splinting ideas to only commercial products. Many times you will be able to improvise splints or supports from things nearby. Once a splint is in place, watch the finished application and make sure the splint holds the limb securely. If it can move or does not immobilize the necessary area, you must try something else.

Boards, Branches, Skis. Boards, branches, skis and other stiff objects are obvious splints in the wilderness. Using these types of solid objects is not as simple as it appears, however. Attaching the branch or ski so that it provides a secure, solid immobilization is difficult. The splint must be wrapped, taped, wired, or tied tight enough to provide a solid attachment. Solid board, branches or skis do not conform to the shape of the body and create pressure points that can become painful, especially with movement.

I prefer to use solid splints only if the body is padded. This can be done by applying the splint over the clothing, wrapping the splint with cloth, and placing padding as necessary. Padding can be other cloth items or wadded paper.

Buddy Taping/Wrapping. Buddy taping is a good means to splint. This is when you wrap or tape the injured finger or limb to the good finger or limb. For example, you can tape a broken finger to a good finger right next to it, using the good finger as a splint. Likewise, a broken arm can be taped or wrapped to the torso, and a broken leg can be taped or wrapped to the other leg.

Pillows. Pillows make excellent splints. Place a pillow around the injured area, then tape or tie it tightly with strips of cloth. The cradling of the injury will often feel good to the patient. Pillow splints can also be taped or tied to other uninjured parts of the body for additional support.

Blankets. A blanket can be used to splint a broken leg. Lay a blanket on the ground and fold it lengthwise until the blanket is the width of the desired length of the splint. At each side of the blanket, roll the material towards the middle, making a "scroll" type configuration. Unroll the two halves slightly and lay the injured limb between the two rolls, which will cradle and support the injured limb. Then tape, wrap, or tie the blanket around the entire leg.

Depending on the blanket, it may or may not be stiff enough to provide adequate splinting. If additional stiffness is needed, you can roll sticks or other straight, stiff objects into the blanket roll. The blanket roll spreads the pressure along the entire leg and makes the patient more comfortable.

USING A BLANKET AND STICKS TO MAKE A LEG SPLINT

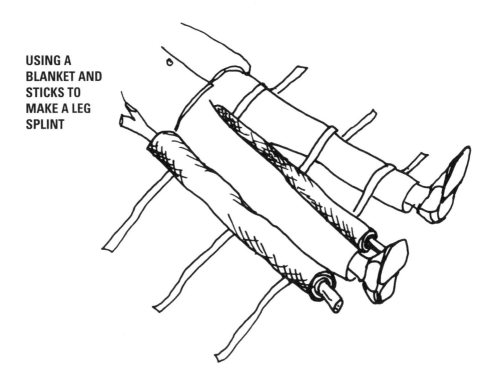

Cloth Rolls. A simple splint for hand injuries is a cloth roll. Simply put the roll in the palm of the hand and tape or wrap the entire hand.

Duct Tape. Duct tape (or any kind of tape) is very handy for splinting. Tape must be used correctly, however, so it does not cause further damage. Taping a broken finger, broken arm, or broken leg is very easy. The main problem with using tape is that if the tape is applied directly to the skin, the only way to remove it is by pulling or through some tedious chemical application. Some tapes have very strong, sticky adhesives that become stronger the longer they are applied. When splinting with tape, try to avoid direct contact with the skin.

A simple way to avoid the skin is to first cover the area with cloth. Socks (the patient's or your own) are excellent for this purpose. Cut the sock as necessary to fit the injury. Then apply the tape over the sock so that it sticks to the cloth, not directly to the skin. With this method, a doctor can cut away the tape without moving the injury unnecessarily. Tee shirts, a leg from a pair of pants, a towel, a bandanna, etc. can all be used to first cover the injury.

Great care must be taken so as not to apply the tape too tightly. It is of utmost importance to maintain circulation to the injury and to areas below the injury. The tendency is to pull tape off the roll, pulling against the attached portion. However, this will pull the applied tape too tightly. Pull tape off the roll by holding back with your other hand, not against the injury.

Also be careful that the tape you use will not shrink after application. Electrical and vinyl tapes stretch when pulled off the roll. After application, they will slowly contract back to their original length. As a result, you may have applied the tape to an injury at an appropriate tension that allowed circulation, but the constriction might tighten it and cut off circulation.

Cardboard. Cardboard makes a very good splint. If you have a corrugated box, you can often cut a piece large enough to wrap around the broken limb. Fold the cardboard in the same direction as the corrugation, then place the injured limb in the fold. Wrap the cardboard with tape or tie it with strips of cloth. If necessary, you might want to put padding (rolls of cloth or wadded up paper) inside the cardboard to create a more supporting fit. Cardboard can also be fashioned as a shielding cover to protect a patient's broken ribs.

SLINGS

Another form of immobilization is the sling. Slings have application for any arm injury and are also useful with rib injuries. They can be fashioned out of any cloth, bandanna, belt, or tape that will support the arm. When securing an arm in a sling, the wrist should be higher than the elbow.

Injured ribs can be very painful. Often splinting the arm on the side of

85

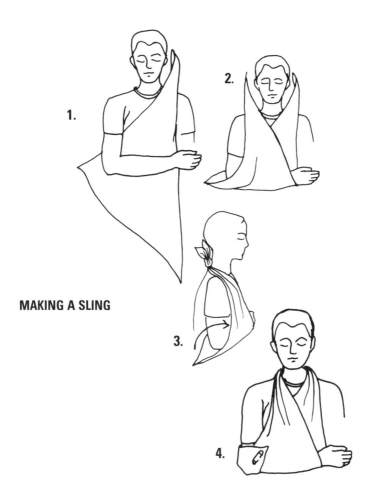

MAKING A SLING

the injured rips can provide relief. It often helps the patient to cover the injured side with the folded arm and tape or sling the arm into place. The arm protects the injured area.

QUICK NECK AND UPPER BACK IMMOBILIZATION

One very dangerous condition to an injured person is inadequate neck immobilization. However, there are cases in which a patient must be moved immediately to save their life. For example, a patient has just fallen in a manner that very possibly has injured his neck and upper back. He has landed in a creek bed and must be moved out of the water. Or perhaps a victim has just been in a rollover car accident. They were ejected and laying right next to the vehicle. The car is now on fire, and starting to burn rapidly. You can safely get to the person now, but realize that in a couple of minutes the vehicle will be an inferno.

What technique could you use to quickly move the patient a minimum distance to safety and yet offer the neck and upper back some protection?

You must realize that improper movement of a victim such as this could easily cause them to be paralyzed for the rest of their lives, yet failure to move them could mean death.

Using a blanket, sheet, or large piece of cloth of any kind you can make a very quick C-collar. Carefully support the neck and head with your hands or knees. Place the blanket around the back of the neck as if you were putting on a scarf. Wrap the blanket around the head and cross it in front over the chest, again like you would wear a scarf. Then continue the ends of the blanket under the armpits, and under the shoulders. The tails of the blanket will be under the patient, coming back toward the head. You can then drag the patient by the blanket tails to a safer location.

Moving the patient in this manner is fast and offers limited neck and upper back immobilizations. Practicing this technique is easy, and you will see how well it works and how quickly you can set it up. Having this done to you will demonstrate how securely it will support your head and upper back very quickly. Dragging a patient is not usually preferred, but getting the patient out of harm's way is often more urgent.

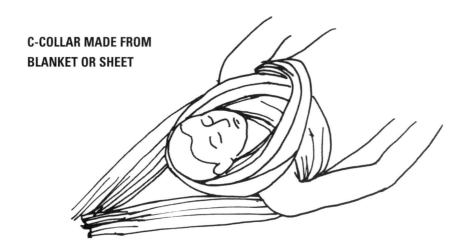

**C-COLLAR MADE FROM
BLANKET OR SHEET**

This same blanket wrap around the neck can be used as an immobilization of the head, neck and upper back even if you do not move the patient. Wrap the head and neck under the armpits as above, then tie or tape the wrap into place.

IMPALED OBJECTS

Never attempt to remove an impaled object. This is a job for surgeons, in a controlled setting, to minimize additional damage and bleeding. The best thing for you to do is stabilize the injury and wait for assistance.

Transporting the Injured

Transporting an injured person is not a simple matter. Most wilderness injuries happen at a considerable distance from the road, over poorly accessible or difficult terrain. Trails are often narrow, rocky, muddy, steep or otherwise difficult. To move a person by carrying them requires a considerable amount of manpower and is very slow. If you cannot move a person out of the wilderness or if moving him or her would possibly cause further injury, you must stabilize the person as well as you can, then go seek help, or wait for help to arrive, depending on the circumstances.

Communication is very important while transporting an injured person. Hearing him or her talk is an excellent indicator of mental alertness. Either you or the patient talking also reduces the anxiety they feel. Explaining what is happening, when to expect a bump, telling them they are going to be just fine — any comforting conversation will help.

If you have a four-wheeler, snowmobile, or sled, use it, but only if you are sure of your destination, and confident that moving your companion won't cause further injury. If you're not certain whether to move someone, stay put, and do your best to make yourself and them comfortable.

Head Injuries

As you care for any obvious injury, look for signs of a head injury. Talk to the person. Are they coherent? Do they remember how it happened? If they do not, he or she may have a head injury. Do they know what day it is? What month? Make them tell you. Ask them if they know where they are. Ask them to tell you who is the current president? Listen for coherent answers.

Patients with head injuries can sound relatively coherent. They can often respond to questions and maintain their composure for quite some time.

It is also not uncommon for patients with head injuries to go into a "fight or flight" mode. A person will either instinctively run from the accident or become combative. Watch for signs of combativeness — it could be a sign that things are changing in their brain. These symptoms are instinctive and cannot be controlled by the patient. The rescuers must also be aware of the combative person for their own safety. These people are not themselves — often they are feeling no pain and they cannot be reasoned with, although you should try. They believe they are fighting for survival and can be difficult to restrain.

Immobilization of the head, neck and upper back, along with the application of oxygen, usually a high rate of flow by mask, is the most appropriate treatment for a head injury. Higher levels of oxygen help reduce or prevent brain swelling. Obviously, oxygen is not available in the wilderness, so you should instead do what you can to keep the patient calm and immobilized.

. . . never assume an injured person has been drinking. Head injuries, hypo/hyper-glycemic reactions, and some allergic reactions can all give the appearance of intoxication.

Use the C-collar to immobilize the head and neck as described earlier. You can also place a rolled towel or cloth under the neck to support it and two sturdy object on either side of the head to keep it stable until help arrives. It is also wise to treat for shock by slightly elevating the head and keeping the patient warm.

Feel the neck while keeping it immobile and look for any signs of tenderness or pain. The slightest sign of pain or tenderness should be a red flag that this may be a serious injury. Check for bruising behind the ears and between the ear and what feels like the edge of the skull. Look for bruising around the eyes (raccoon eyes). Check for any fluid in the ears, and whether it is clear or not. If the fluid is yellowish, lay the person down and let it drain out.

The skull is a very complex structure with many fragile parts. Any impact could fracture the more delicate, interior bones that support the brain. The skull has areas with high blood circulation. Bleeding as a result of damage to any portion of the head can cause pressure on the brain. The brain might not be injured as a result of the initial impact, but bleeding and internal pressures could result in a progressive injury. This might account for the patient who appears all right during the initial assessment and then progressively worsens. Any progressive change in the person's alertness, personality, eye appearance, or they experience nausea, may be signs that brain injury has occured.

NEVER ASSUME

If you meet up with an injured person and he or she appears to be incoherent or drunk, never assume the person has been drinking or taking drugs. Head injuries, hypo/hyperglycemic reactions, and some allergic reactions can all give the appearance of intoxication.

Even if a person is intoxicated and is injured, the injuries can be quite extensive. Alcohol and other drugs will mask pain and other symptoms. Patients involved in accidents that are influenced by these chemicals can have extensive internal damage. Alcohol and drug related accidents are not uncommon in wilderness settings. People often "let their hair down" while in the backcountry, perhaps feeling "freer" in the wilderness.

Snake Bites

Snakes have a terrible (and undeserved) reputation. Rather than the fearsome, poisonous creatures they are believed to be, they are instead colorful, beautiful animals that make a significant contribution to our environment. Snakes are, in fact, very fearful animals. They do not want confrontation; they want to get away from you. The only reason they become aggressive is because they feel trapped, their escape routes are blocked, or they feel they do not have enough space to get away. The snake might attack in self-defense, but not aggressively.

If you have a confrontation with a snake of any kind, back off and give it some room. More than likely the snake will leave. Snakes are cold-blooded reptiles. They are active in warm weather and hibernate in cold conditions. The best way to avoid a snake encounter is to understand their habits and habitats. If you are in snake country, be aware of the temperature. If it is cool and the sun is shining, snakes may be found lying in the sun trying to warm up, especially in rocky areas. If it is hot, they might be in dens, beneath shady bushes, or under rocky outcroppings trying to stay cool.

Farmers and ranchers have long known that if you are picking up a hay bale, always tip it toward you in case a rattler is lying under it. In tipping it toward you, the bottom of the bale is open on the side away from you, giving the snake an escape route. The same technique is applicable in the wilderness. If you are moving logs, rocks, or other objects that might be the temporary shelter of a snake, tip it toward you, giving the snake a chance to escape.

Occasionally a person will accidentally startle a snake that attacks in self-defense. There are very few, truly poisonous snakes in the U.S. or even the world. In the U.S., the two types of snakes that are poisonous are the "pit vipers" and the coral snake. Pit vipers include the variety of rattlesnakes, the water moccasin, and copperheads. In the U.S. annually, there are approximately 40,000 to 50,000 snake bites reported; of these approximately 7,000 are caused by poisonous snakes, and of these, only about 15 cases are fatal.

Most snakes are non-venomous, including the common bull snake and garter snake. These snakes will strike an intruder in self-defense, however, often with the appearance of a rattler or coral snake. Their bites could cause infection, but not death.

The public has an overwhelming fear of snakes, thinking that any bite will surely prove fatal. Years ago the thinking was to place a tourniquet on the limb, cut slits in the fang marks, then suck the blood and poison from the bite. Cutting and sucking on snakebite wounds is no longer considered appropriate treatment. It has been proven that there are very few cases in which the snake is able to inject a fatal dose of poison. It has also been proven that the snake injects what poison is available too deeply into the flesh to be effectively removed by sucking.

If a snake bites you or someone you are with, don't panic. Remember that many snake bites are non-poisonous. If you are bitten by a rattle or coral snake, do not panic. Many of the poisonous snake are unable to inject a fatal amount of poison.

If you can, capture or kill the snake for later identification. If it proves to be a poisonous snake, identification of the specific species will be necessary for determining the correct anti-venom.

IN CASE OF POISONOUS SNAKE BITE:

1. *Stay calm and keep the patient lying down. The quieter you stay, the less you will spread the poison through the blood system.*

2. *Clean the wound with soap and copious amounts of water. The use of an antiseptic will help prevent infection.*

3. *Place a restriction above the bitten area — a constrictive band, belt, or other restriction that resembles a tourniquet around the limb. Unlike a tourniquet, this is not intended to shut down arterial circulation. You want to slow the venous circulation, which will carry the poison back into the body, but you do not want to interfere with deeper arterial circulation. After application of the restriction, you should be able to feel a pulse in the extremity below the bite.*

4. *Splint the bitten limb to prevent movement. Watch the victim carefully, monitoring the vital signs.*

5. *Elevate the legs, treating for shock and keeping the patient warm.*

6. *Transport the patient as soon as possible.*

7. *Do not allow the patient to eat.*

8. *Be careful if the patient vomits. Aspiration of vomit is as much a threat as is the poison. It is common for a patient to vomit as a result of anxiety or fear of dying, and not because of the poison.*

9. *Do not give the patient any alcohol.*

Staying calm and keeping those with you calm is the most important action. The more excited the patient, the faster the poison will be circulated through the body. Getting medical attention as soon as possible is also very important. I have known many individuals who have been bitten by rattlesnakes. None of those individuals died. A few became ill, others became very sick, but all fully recovered.

Hypothermia

Hypothermia is a condition in which the body temperature falls into a sub-normal range and cannot recover without the addition of heat from an outside source. The body cannot produce heat fast enough to overcome the lower temperature. Hypothermia is an extremely dangerous situation that must be recognized, treated, and controlled in its early stages before it is too late.

Hypothermia can occur in only a few seconds in certain conditions, such as falling into an icy lake, or it can happen gradually, almost unnoticeably, by long exposure to a cool or cold environment. Hypothermia can happen anytime the body is exposed to temperatures that are below 98.6 degrees.

The risk of hypothermia is compounded by dehydration and extreme physical stress. Dehydration lessens the body's ability to circulate heat efficiently, while physical stress depletes the body of normal energy reserves that are used to maintain normal temperature.

Insulating a hypothermic person with clothing, sleeping bags, or other methods will slow or stop the heat loss, but the body cannot increase its temperature. The only way to increase their temperature is by adding heat from an outside source.

WARNING SIGNS OF HYPOTHERMIA

The body automatically takes action to protect the vital organs. The limbs are a much lower priority to maintain life, so the body begins a "shunting process," or a constriction of the blood vessels in the limbs to keep the body heat (blood) in the core of the body and brain areas. This shunting is a gradual process that starts in the extremities and works toward the trunk of the body.

As circulation is being shunted to the more vital parts of the body, you will notice your extremities becoming increasingly colder and numb. This starts with the fingertips and tips of your toes and progressively works up your limbs. These may be the first signs that you are heading toward hypothermia.

Normal body temperature is 98.6 degrees. When it drops below this, your body recognizes it and starts using muscles and energy reserves in an attempt to generate heat. Involuntary shivering is simply the muscles trying to convert their energy reserves into heat. Involuntary shivering is the second sign that your body is becoming increasingly colder.

Shivering becomes more severe as the body temperature drops. Shivering is not controllable and is a very obvious sign that a person needs to get warmer. If you notice a companion shivering uncontrollably, you must take action for that person.

When your body temperature drops to 95-96 degrees, the shivering becomes extremely violent. You will no longer be able to think clearly. You will become more and more forgetful. Your speech, coordination, and movement will become more difficult. You may begin to experience bouts of amnesia. At this point, you would barely have the presence of mind to remedy the situation on your own.

When your body temperature drops to 95-96 degrees, the shivering becomes extremely violent. You will no longer be able to think clearly.

When your body temperature drops to 90 degrees, the shivering will stop. Your thinking is now very unclear. The amnesia becomes more pronounced. You may start to experience hallucinations, feelings of claustrophobia, paranoia, uncontrolled panic, muscle spasms, and rigidity of your muscles. Your movements are more difficult and jerky. Your body color begins to take on a bluish tint. You can stand and walk, but aimlessly.

When your body temperature drops to 86 degrees, you will be unconscious as all reflexes become depressed. As the body temperature drops to 78 degrees, death usually occurs.

TREATING HYPOTHERMIA

Hypothermia must be treated at the first signs. As you review the progressive description, notice that the body experiences diminished mental ability soon after the first signs of shivering. This is a progressive, life-threatening situation that must be dealt with immediately because it escalates at an alarming rate.

Anyone with advanced hypothermia — anything beyond shivering or any diminished mental ability — should be transported to an emergency medical facility as soon as possible. Since you may be in a wilderness survival situation, you may not have that option. You will need to treat yourself or your companion immediately.

Treatment consists of two steps: 1) stop further heat loss 2) add warmth safely to the body to reverse the effects.

STOP THE HEAT LOSS

The first step in treating hypothermia is to stop the heat loss. This might include making a shelter, using extra clothing, removing wet clothing, getting out of the wind, or any other action to stop more heat from leaving the body. Review the way heat is transferred from the body: evaporation, radiation, convection, and conduction.

Evaporation. Heat loss by evaporation is one area that is often overlooked until it is too late. Wet clothes can result from snow, rain, falling into water, or perspiring in cool temperatures. Wet clothing must be removed and replaced with dry clothing on a hypothermic person. The ability to start a fire and dry clothing can be a matter of life and death. A large fire might work to dry clothing while still on your body. If you have dressed in layers you may be able to build a large fire, remove some layers, dry them out, then trade those dry layers for damp ones. Choose clothing that dries quickly and maintains insulation values when wet (see last chapter).

Convection. Convection is heat loss by air movement. Getting out of the wind alone might make enough of a difference to stop the progression of hypothermia. Heat loss through convection can be tremendous especially when there is also evaporation. If you stand in a breeze while you are damp in sub-freezing temperatures, you can be dead in minutes. A windbreak is any object that stops the wind.

Radiation. Your body radiates heat if it is not covered with insulation. Insulation includes clothing, a sleeping bag, blankets, shelters, gloves, hat, etc. The head radiates a very high percentage of the total body heat, yet it is one area that is often left exposed. Some people just can't stand to wear a hat or helmet, or their head never feels cold so they just leave it off. You must stop all heat from leaving the body, which includes the head. Cover the head and save that heat for the rest of the body.

Conduction. Objects with two different temperatures that touch will transfer heat from the warmer object to the colder. If you sit on a cold rock, your behind becomes cold as the heat from your body tries to heat that rock. You must insulate any direct contact with any object that is colder than your body.

ADDING WARMTH TO THE BODY

Along with stopping any additional heat from leaving the body, you must add heat to reverse the process. Depending on the level of hypothermia, adding heat can be very dangerous if not done correctly.

If the victim is conscious and capable of drinking fluids on their own, give that person warm fluids. At this stage, hypothermia is relatively easy to reverse. If you don't have warm fluids, a campfire or climbing into a sleeping bag or blankets with another person will reverse hypothermia.

DANGERS INVOLVED WITH ADVANCED HYPOTHERMIA

A person who has advanced hypothermia is clinging to life. This is an extremely fragile condition that can lead to cardiac failure. The situation is so sensitive that EMT's are not allowed to use any type of artificial airway in the mouth or nose, since just tripping the gag reflex in the throat can cause cardiac arrest.

Stop the heat loss immediately and remove that person from the cold environment. Remove cold wet clothes and replace them with dry clothes. If you have a sleeping bag, take off both their clothes and yours and crawl in with them. This is not a time to be shy or modest; someone's life is at stake, and clothing insulates both bodies and hinders heat transfer.

The adding of heat must be done gradually and very carefully. As the body was cooled down from the extremities to the core, it is vital to warm it back up from the core to the extremities. The body shunted its blood and fluids from the extremities, leaving those extremities without circulation and heat for the longest period of time. Remaining blood and fluids in the extremities will be much colder than the core temperature.

Heat must be added to the core, allowing it to satisfy those temperature demands and naturally begin circulation in other less critical parts of the body. Do not attempt to warm any hypothermia victim by applying heat to any extremity until that person is conscious, alert, and able to take fluids on their own!

Since the extremities are significantly colder than the core, any premature circulation can pump cold fluids into the internal organs and lower core temperature. The additional stress on the heart caused by the temperature drop and the additional fluids that now will be in circulation, along with the additional areas now needing circulation, could cause a fatal cardiac overload.

RE-HEATING THE BODY SAFELY

Re-heating the body is a very slow process. In cases I have seen, doctors raise the body temperature at a rate of one degree per hour. This rate allows the body to gradually recover and begin circulation without causing additional stress to the organs.

Warmth must be added to the body at the core. External application of heat packs or other heat sources must be done to areas that have high circulation, and go directly to the core organs. Good areas to put heat packs are along the neck, in the armpits, and over the kidneys. These areas have relatively little muscle and body fat to hamper heat transfer, and have high circulation.

A person in advanced hypothermia will not feel pain. You must be careful that you do not apply too much heat and burn them.

As the body temperature rises, the person will begin to regain normal body functions. Only give warm fluids when the person is conscious and able to drink on their own. That person must be protected from heat loss or any physical exertion until they have comfortably returned to normal body temperatures.

Frostbite

The human body is a marvelous creation. When in distress, it takes measures to preserve its primary organs. When the circulatory system begins shunting body heat from the extremities to the core of the body (such as described in hypothermia), fingers, toes, hands and feet are often cold and more susceptible to freezing. Ears, noses, cheeks and other exposed flesh are also subject to frostbite in extreme cold.

Frostbite is a very serious injury. It is the result of cells of the flesh freezing. Frozen cells expand, rupture, change chemically, and are otherwise ruined by the frostbite. Severe damage to the flesh is a result. The degree of damage is similar to a burn; the deeper the flesh is frozen, the more severe the injury. Superficial frostbite appears white or grayish, and the skin is usually cold, numb and extremely painful. Deeper, more serious frostbite is white skin that is hard and lacks feeling.

In extreme frostbite, the damaged cells can die. If enough damage is done, the flesh will develop gangrene (dead flesh still attached to the body). Amputation is often necessary. In many cases in which the person has refused amputation, the toes or fingers will rot and fall off, subjecting the patient to an increased chance of infection.

TREATING FROSTBITE

Frostbite is an injury that may be treated differently in every case. If at all possible, transport the patient to the nearest medical facility. In a wilderness survival setting, that may not be possible. You may be required to treat the patient in the field.

First, remove the patient from the cold environment as much as possible. You must stop any additional injury. Protect the frostbitten areas with clean, sterile dressings if available. Remove any wet or damp clothing. Protect the damaged area from cold. Be careful not to bump, touch, or rub the frozen part. Never rub a frostbitten area in an effort to warm it up.

Never rub a frostbitten area in an effort to warm it up. Rubbing will destroy the frozen flesh, which is now cells made up of ice crystals.

Rubbing will destroy the frozen flesh, which is now cells made up of ice crystals. Rubbing is also ineffective in getting warmth below the surface of the flesh.

Warming a frostbitten person is difficult. From reading the information on hypothermia you will understand how dangerous it is to warm the body incorrectly. If the patient has frostbite, they will usually be in some state of hypothermia. Treat the hypothermia as a priority, and the frostbite injury as a lower priority.

Do not attempt to warm any frostbitten part if there is any chance that the part will be re-frozen, or if you are unable to protect it from the cold. Once an area is frozen, the damage is done; significantly more damage results from a freeze-thaw-freeze-thaw process. People have been known to walk on frostbitten feet and use frostbitten hands without significant additional damage. Once a foot or hand has been thawed, it must be protected — it is not useable.

Do not warm the extremity by fire or hot exhaust. The patient will not be able to feel the heat, which could cause further damage. The best method is to use a water bath with the water temperature between 100 and 112 degrees. Damage to the cells will result if the water is more than 112 degrees. Keep the parts submerged in the water until all the cold is gone. It is a difficult, long, slow process and is very painful for the patient. As the warmth comes back into the extremity, so does the feeling.

Once you thaw the parts, it is of utmost importance to protect the injury and prevent further freezing. Properly thawing a frostbitten body part is such a difficult and dangerous procedure in the field that I recommend it only be attempted in extreme circumstances.

Heat Exhaustion

Heat exhaustion is a condition where the body's cooling ability has been impaired by dehydration, low electrolyte levels, or the inability of the body to cool itself through perspiration. The body normally reduces its temperature by perspiring. Evaporation of the perspiration cools the body efficiently.

Heat exhaustion can occur if a person is over-dressed, but it is more commonly caused by dehydration. When a person is dehydrated and still exerting physical effort or in hot conditions, the body is unable to perspire or remove the heat from vital organs through adequate circulation. The condition of reduced body fluid volume, primarily blood fluid, is called hypovolemia (low volume).

As the body overheats, the patient might experience weakness, dizziness, nausea, and headache. They may even faint. Their skin might feel cold and clammy, and they will have a rapid pulse as the heart tries to circulate heat away from the internal organs.

The patient is experiencing a mild form of "hypovolemic shock." The appropriate action is to remove them from the source of heat. In a wilderness environment, it might be moving into the shade, getting out into a breeze, or removing clothing so that air can contact the skin. It is also extremely important to replenish the body fluids and electrolytes. The commercial drinks that restore electrolytes work very well, but drinking plain water will often make a tremendous difference.

The patient will usually fully recover within 30 minutes if the fluids are restored.

Heat Stroke

Heat stroke is a much more serious degree of overheating. This is a life-threatening situation because the body is now overheated to a point where cells are dying. The situation is similar to heat exhaustion but the degree of damage is much more severe. Transportation to a medical facility is required for heat stroke victims.

Heat stroke is an urgent emergency. The amount of time it takes you to cool the patient could determine the difference between life and death. The patient must be removed from the heat immediately. If available, ice the body down. If water is available in limited amounts, use wet cloths and mop the body. The clothing must be removed to allow as much heat to escape as possible. If you have unlimited amounts of water, such as a nearby stream, pour water on the person or put him or her directly in the water (although do not put the person in icy water). The body temperature must be brought down.

Never attempt to give an unconscious person any fluids. The risk of aspiration is great and could cause tremendous problems. If the person regains consciousness, give fluids liberally. If the person is able to swallow without choking and if they are able to hold a cup on their own, they will be conscious enough to drink fluids without problem. If the body temperature is successfully lowered, continue to re-hydrate the person until completely recovered.

Shock

Shock occurs when the body cannot perfuse the various organs, muscles, and tissues with enough blood.

There are three basic causes of shock:
1. The heart is compromised or damaged, and unable to adequately circulate enough blood. This can be caused by heart attack, injury, or any medical or traumatic situation in which the heart is compromised.
2. The volume of blood is reduced through severe bleeding or dehydration to a point that there is not enough fluid left for the body to properly function.
3. The dilation of the blood vessels. The blood vessels control blood pressure by expanding and contracting to maintain the appropriate pressure. If your blood pressure is low, the vessels contract and push the pressure up. If your pressure is too high, they expand and allow the pressure to drop. If the tightness of your vessels is allowed to relax, without enough fluid volume, the pressure will drop very low, leaving your circulation system unable to perfuse the organs.

The medical types of shock are categorized as hypovolemic, anaphylactic, metabolic, neurogenic, psychogenic, cardiogenic, septic and respiratory shock. I've briefly describe each type of shock:

Hypovolemic or Hemorrhagic Shock. A shock caused by low blood volume. Common to extreme dehydration, severe blood loss, or fluid loss caused by severe burns.

Anaphylactic Shock. Shock caused by a severe allergic reaction. With this type of shock, the body has not lost blood or fluids, and there are no circulation problems. Fluids instead build in the lungs and bronchi tubes drowning the patient. In some cases, the throat swells and respiration is hindered. The inability of the body to absorb oxygen causes the shock. This type of shock is common with bee stings, bug bites, food reactions and other severe allergic reactions.

Metabolic Shock. Shock caused by illness in which the patient has become dehydrated through loss of body fluids caused by diarrhea, vomiting, urination, or similar.

Neurogenic Shock. Shock caused by the loss of control of the blood vessels as a result of nerve damage. This loss of control allows the blood vessels to dilate, causing the blood pressure to drop dangerously. This is the type of shock caused by a broken neck or other nerve injuries.

Psychogenic Shock. A type of shock caused by a sudden reaction of the nervous system. For example, if you stand up quickly, you might feel light headed and faint. Fainting due to a nervous reaction to a situation is this type of shock. It happens briefly because once you fall, you are prostrate, allowing the blood to circulate back into the brain.

Cardiogenic Shock. Shock caused by ineffective cardiac output. This can be a result of heart attack, heart disease, poor circulation, or any other number of reasons. Blood pressure might be too low, or the heart rate not fast enough.

Septic Shock. This shock is caused by the buildup of poisons or toxins in the body, which can cause severe bacterial infections. The poisons can deteriorate the blood vessels and allow the blood to leak into the body. The resulting low fluid causes a hypovolemic shock.

Respiratory Shock. Shock caused by the inadequate operation of the respiratory system. The blood cannot pick up oxygen, so it cannot perfuse the body. This type of shock can be caused by choking or any similar respiratory problem.

Although all of these types of shock are different, they have common signs and symptoms. A person experiencing shock will be restless and anxious. They may have a weak or rapid pulse, and they may feel cold and clammy. The patient could exhibit heavy sweating, and might appear pale, even taking on a bluish tint as the oxygen levels fall. Their breathing can become labored as the person attempts to put more oxygen into their body. The eyes might become vacant, dull in appearance, reacting slowly or not at all to light. The patient could be very thirsty as his body demands fluids. Nausea and vomiting could also be present. The blood pressure drops to a dangerously low level. The patient might lose consciousness.

One obvious sign of shock is when the heart rate increases while the blood pressure drops. The heart tries to compensate for the low output by working harder, yet there is nothing left to pump.

TREATMENT FOR SHOCK

Shock is a life-threatening crisis and must be treated immediately. It is best if you know why the person is in this condition, but there are common procedures that can be followed even if you don't know the reason.

Maintain the respiratory system. This means maintaining an airway and performing rescue breathing if necessary. Keep the mouth and airway clear of obstructions. Provide oxygen if you have some available. Do not give the patient anything by mouth. The threat of aspiration into the lungs is too great to chance.

Control any bleeding or other fluid loss. If the person is bleeding, do what it takes to keep bleeding under control. If the fluid loss is due to heat and perspiration, move the patient and cool them.

Keep the patient lying down and calm. Do not allow any exertion by the patient.

Elevate the feet and legs slightly above the level of the heart, unless the patient has a head injury. A common position used in EMT is called the "Trendelenburg position." This is when a patient is on their back with their feet elevated approximately six inches. The fluids in the legs will be moved by gravity into the core of the body and brain.

Keep careful record of the patient's vital signs, the breaths per minute and the heart rate, along with the blood pressure if possible. Monitor them every five minutes so that you will be aware if the patient worsens.

Seek medical help if at all possible. It is rare that you will be able to successfully treat for shock without help from a doctor. If someone is with you, consider sending someone for help.

Shock is a life threatening medical emergency. Although the shock is caused by other injuries, sickness or trauma, shock is responsible for many deaths. The need to obtain first aid training cannot be stressed enough. Your local ambulance, fire department, hospital or schools will direct you to the available classes. A few hours invested now might save a loved one later. Make the investment; you will be glad you did.

Keeping a basic first-aid kit in your pack will help you deal with the sorts of injuries that are most likely to occur on a wilderness outing. You will be able to treat minor cuts, blisters, or burns sufficiently to keep them from becoming bigger problems. The larger bandages will help you keep major injuries under control until you can get help.

BASIC FIRST-AID KIT:

There are many first-aid kits available on the market, but you can assemble as good or a better one on your own. The following are the minimum items that should be contained in your kit.

- [ ] adhesive bandages of varying sizes to keep small cuts clean and to cover blisters
- [ ] sterile gauze dressing and gauze bandages for larger wounds and burns
- [ ] elastic bandage for sprains or for keeping limbs immobilized
- [ ] ibuprofin or asperin for swelling and pain relief
- [ ] antiseptic cream or ointment
- [ ] antiseptic wipes
- [ ] a small pair of quality scissors
- [ ] safety pins
- [ ] corn pads and foot felt for blisters and other foot problems
- [ ] a large square bandage that can be used as a sling or to bandage a wound.

6
What To Do When You're Lost

One winter, we were called to begin a search for a hunter who had not returned to camp as planned. I was in a Bell 47 helicopter as a spotter, along with the pilot. The ground was covered with snow. Ground teams had picked up the man's tracks and advised us of the direction of travel. We flew over the area and soon picked up his tracks about two miles from the camp. We began tracking the person by flying directly over the tracks, just above treetop level. Because of the remoteness of the location, we were reasonably certain that our lost person had made these tracks.

The tracks showed a normal, evenly-spaced stride going up and down hills. We followed the tracks and spotted two places where the person had stopped to make yellow snow. Yellow snow is a very good sign because it tells the searcher that the person is still healthy and hydrated. These marks are easy to spot because a person will usually step off the trail to urinate rather than urinate on the trail.

At the three- to four-mile point, we began to notice the stride length becoming more uneven. The subject began to walk around objects that he would have walked over earlier. We also noticed marks where he had sat down, and we no longer saw any urination marks. The direction of travel had also changed from tracks going from point to point directly, to meandering and winding loops. On occasion, the tracks would double back and cross themselves.

The trail was now at the four- to five-mile mark. The tracks were much more erratic in spacing. You could see the person was now exhausted, probably dehydrated, becoming hypothermic and limping. His path no longer made sense. He would avoid even the simplest and smallest obstacles. His steps changed from normal to one that obviously favored his heel, usually a sign of numb or frozen toes.

He began to use his rifle as a walking stick; we could see the marks of his rifle butt and sling in the snow. A hunter usually considers his rifle a prized possession. He would never use the rifle this way unless he has given up on the hunt, realizing the seriousness of the situation.

From this point on, we never noticed any sit down marks. This, combined with the erratic track, is common when panic and hopelessness overwhelms a person. They reason that if they stop they will never start up again.

At the five-mile mark, we noticed gear being discarded. This is an extremely serious situation that we often see. This indicates that hypothermia is to the point that the person is losing mental awareness. Hypothermia victims will often feel burdened by gear or feel claustrophobic and discard gear. This usually indicates the search will end in a body recovery. We observed the gear that was left and noticed it was very selective, which gave us hope.

Shortly following this point we found a sit down mark. The subject found a walking stick and was no longer using his rifle. His course now became much more defined.

In later interviews, he told us that he knew he was lost at the two-mile mark, where we had started tracking him. However, it was at the five- to six-mile point that he had finally come to grips with his situation. He realized that either he would get control of his panic and start using common sense or he would surely die. Interviews also later revealed that he was mentally in control at all times and had methodically gone through his pack and discarded any unnecessary weight. He had sat at the five-mile mark location for several minutes, rested and then continued on a much more defined course.

At the five- to seven-mile point we noticed he was attempting to get up to a vantage point. His course was much better defined as he was making a substantial effort to get to a higher elevation. The effort was impressive, but he gave it up when he physically could not go any higher.

In an open area he tramped out the word "HELP" in twenty-foot letters and an arrow pointing to the direction he would be traveling. From that point he only traveled downhill, obviously exhausted. At the seven-

If you get lost, follow these rules:

1. Admit to yourself that you're lost.

2. Stop traveling.

3. Stay calm and think positive.

4. Make or find shelter.

5. Gather firewood.

6. Make a fire while you're waiting to be found.

and-one-half-mile point, it was apparent he was slipping into severe hypothermia. He discarded his rifle and his course once again became irrational.

We spotted him at a point eight miles from his starting point. He was nearly unconscious, had frostbitten hands and feet, and little gear left. He had spent two nights outside. He recovered from the hypothermia but lost all toes on one foot, three toes on the other foot, and three fingers.

STAY CALM AND STAY PUT

The best survivalists, navigators, skiers, snowmobilers or woodsmen have all been lost, and they will either admit to it or lie about it. I have gotten lost on many occasions, including while on searches for others who were lost. How you deal with being lost can result in an emergency or a temporary inconvenience.

If you realize you are lost, what is the best thing you can do? Do you have the navigational skills to locate and pinpoint yourself on a map and do you know how to use a compass? Do you have a map and compass?

The first thing you must do is stop traveling. If you don't know where you are now, moving will only distance you from familiar territory.

Stay calm. Being lost is not the end of the world. You might feel insecure because you do not know the direction to go for safety, but you can minimize the danger if you use your head. Panic will only make you use poor judgement.

Sit down, take a break, and try to relax. Clear your mind of any anxiety and think of where you have traveled. Retrace your steps in your mind from the last point you knew your location. Often in thinking about the trail, you will remember where you went wrong. If you do recall where you went wrong, you might be able to backtrack to that point.

Keep a positive attitude. Try to laugh at yourself and think "another fine mess I've gotten myself into." Start to think your way through the situation. Stay at your present location for at least thirty minutes, making plans for your next action.

While resting, make a fire. Fire is magical in a survival situation. The physical and mental effort required to build and maintain a fire will keep your mind occupied and distract you from any fear. Once you have a fire lit, you will have a source of heat and a place to dry out your gear. The fire produces smoke which makes a signal for those who will be looking for you. The fire will keep you in one location which will prevent you from getting further lost.

A campfire has a very soothing and calming effect on individuals. The warmth, sounds and light are almost companion-like. Gather your thoughts, gather your resources, and keep your senses. If you stay in control, you will easily be able to care for yourself.

The Four-o'Clock Rule

If it is after four PM and you're unsure of where you are, make plans to spend the night. You will only have a couple of hours of sunlight left to prepare, even in the summertime.

Use your time to gather firewood for the night. Gather as much firewood as you feel you will need to get through the night and then triple that amount. It is very disappointing at midnight to realize you have run out of wood; it is much simpler to gather wood in the light.

While you're at it, gather some fuel that will flare in case you need a signal fire during the night. Reserve this for signaling only. Green, wet material makes excellent smoke for signaling, while dry leaves or pine needles (green or dry) will flare up when put on the fire.

Use your time to construct a shelter. Your shelter type will obviously be determined by the circumstances. If it is summertime and the temperature won't drop much, you may only need a simple lean-to to protect you from the rain. If it is winter, find anyplace dry and out of the wind. A tree well under a large fir tree makes a good shelter in a short amount of time. You have a lot of work to do between four PM and darkness. Building a shelter will be challenging enough in daylight and very difficult in darkness.

Throughout all of these "chores," maintaining a positive mental attitude is the most important thing you can do. Laugh at yourself and consider each challenge an adventure. Think about the story you'll have to tell your friends instead of thinking the worst.

Plan the night by first taking an inventory of your resources. I am not talking only about the things in your pack but also the natural resources that are available. Look at the trees, grasses, rock and snow formations for shelters. Look for pine boughs for your bedding, walls or ceiling. Scout out the immediate area in case you need additional resources during the night. Make mental notes of the area because things will look completely different at night.

If the night is clear, use the stars to your advantage. Try to determine the directions by the stars (discussed later), and verify those directions when the sun rises. If you know the direction you were traveling from the start of your trip, you should be able to get your bearings. What to do in the morning is determined by a number of circumstances: will anyone be reporting you as missing and do they know your destination (stay put); do you have provisions to travel (food and water to keep up your energy, plus additional fire-starting material); how is the weather; how remote are you; etc. If you do decide to leave your campsite, leave some sign indicating your direction of travel, such as a large arrow stamped in the snow or formed by broken pine branches. Leave a note listing your time of departure, route, and intended destination if at all possible. You should also mark your trail by tying flags to branches or breaking branches.

Get Oriented

If you are going into an area for the first time, you should have a feel for the lay of the land. Know the direction the roads travel and their relationship to your location. If the nearby road runs east and west and you are going to be on the north side of the road, traveling south would get you back to the road at some point.

Keep track of several landmarks. Pay attention to how the drainages run in relation to those landmarks. Pay attention to your movements through and around the drainages. Use landmarks both nearby and also at a distance. At night, pay attention to the distant lights on the horizon; you can see city lights or radio tower lights and residences for many miles.

Carry maps of the area and any adjacent area you may venture into. Topographical maps are invaluable and can be purchased at most sporting goods stores. Orient yourself on the map and keep track of your travels. Visit with those who are good with maps and compasses and have them give you lessons. Map and compass work is not that difficult and can be fun once you become comfortable with them (discussed later).

Learn to use navigational tools. Develop your navigational abilities. Learn how to use a compass for direction, and how to triangulate your location with distant landmarks. Learn how to plot your location on a topographical map using those same landmarks. Learn how a GPS (Global Positioning Satellite) system works and how other navigational systems work. Do not become dependent on any single system, however.

The GPS systems now available to the general public offer tremendous advancement in wilderness navigation. These systems can be programmed with very complicated routes. They can be programmed to alarm when you need to change direction, or if you wander even a few degrees off the plotted course, and then tell you which way to go to get back on course. A GPS system is great, but it can be damaged or run out of battery charge, and you will need to know what to do then.

Using a map and compass is a time-tested, reliable system. Maps can tell you what is ahead of you and help you to plan your course around any obstructions. It is true that a compass can give false readings in certain areas and it can be damaged, but a compass is still a great navigational tool.

FINDING THE NORTH STAR

Can you find the North Star at night? It is not the brightest star in the sky, but it can be easily located by its relationship to the Big Dipper constellation. The North Star is not part of the Big Dipper, as many people believe.

Find the Big Dipper in the sky. Three stars make up the handle and four stars make up the ladle or cup. On the cup, align the two stars that make the front edge of the cup, or the furthermost two stars from the handle. Heading in the direction away from the open cup, the North Star is the brightest star that aligns with these two stars.

The North Star is always due north during all seasons of the year. The Big Dipper will rotate in position around the star but the alignment will

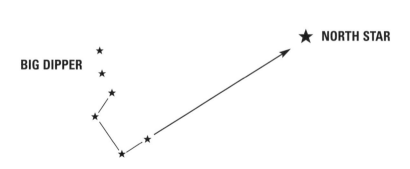

not change. On a clear night, go out and look at the stars to figure it out.

Knowing the directions by the stars is invaluable at times. I was on a search in the mountains one very dark night, riding a four-wheel ATV. We needed to return to the command post, which was several miles away. There were clouds on the horizon and we could not determine mountain shapes to keep our bearings. There was no moon but the rest of the sky was clear. Compasses were difficult to use because we couldn't take bearings from distant objects. We were in heavy timber and could only see what our headlight could reach. We were picking our way through the rocks and trees, making it difficult to keep our bearing, so we used the stars as a reference and traveled directly back to the command post.

Finding the North Star is not difficult and should be practiced before your life depends on it. Practice finding the Big Dipper, the North Star and other constellations. Check yourself out with a compass and see how close you are. Soon you will be comfortable navigating by the North Star.

KEEP TRACK OF YOUR LOCATION

Keep track of your movements on the map, noting the amount of time it takes you to get between points. A good method is to use a pencil and mark an X where you are, writing the time underneath it. It makes a good diary of your travels and also gives you a database for determining a time and distance ratio. If you plot how far you are traveling in a given amount of time, it will help you to determine your location if you are unsure of yourself. For example, if you are averaging one mile per hour and you have been moving for two hours since you last marked your location, you should be about two miles from that last position.

Map and Compass

Understanding and using a map and compass is very simple, but it takes practice. It is not necessary to understand all the latitude and longitude information below to effectively use a map and compass, but the more you understand, the more efficiently you will be able to use your equipment. The more efficiently you use your equipment, the more safety and fun you will experience. It is important that you understand true north, magnetic north, declination, triangulation, plotting information on a map, and then applying that information to a real setting.

To define any location you must have at least three dimensions. When working with maps you use the surface of the earth as one dimension; you must then only define two additional dimensions to specify an exact location. Maps use a grid system to define a specific location; lines running north and south (longitude), and lines running east and west (latitude).

The needle on a compass always points north, but there are two types of north. One north is called true north and the other is magnetic north. There is a significant difference between true and magnetic north, called declination. Your compass points to magnetic north, so you need to make an adjustment on your compass to compensate for the declination, or the difference between magnetic north and the north on your map. A good topo map will tell you what the degree of declination is for the area you're in. As you can see in the map below, it varies depending on where you are.

Declination, western U.S., c. 1995

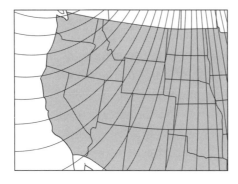
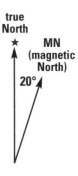

TRUE NORTH

True north is the direction from any point on earth to the North Pole. The North and South Poles pinpoint the axis that the earth rotates on; the equator is the latitude line around the earth that is exactly halfway between the two poles. Most people understand the axis and the equator, but get confused when determining longitude and latitude.

To make things simple, mapmakers have divided the earth into north and south, east and west. From the equator to the North Pole the earth is divided into 90 degrees. 0 degrees is the Equator and 90 degrees is the North Pole; likewise, there are 90 degrees to the South Pole.

LATITUDE

Latitude is the degree of the circle between 0° and 90°, either north or south of the Equator. As an example of how this is defined, the central portion of the United States is approximately 40° north, meaning that this area is north of the Equator about 40 degrees. Central Mexico is approximately 20° North (20° north of the Equator).

> 0° = Equator
> 90°N= North Pole
> 90°S= South Pole
> Central United States is approximately 40°N
> Central Argentina is approximately 40°S

LONGITUDE

The earth is also divided into eastern and western hemispheres. The division is a line of longitude known as the International Date Line on one side of the earth, and the Greenwich Meridian on the other side of the earth.

Just as the Equator divides the earth into north and south halves, or top and bottom using 0 to 90°, Greenwich Meridian is the line used to define east and west. This line runs from the North Pole to the South Pole approximately near London, England. On the opposite side of the earth from the North Pole to the South Pole is the International Date Line. Everything east of the Greenwich Meridian to the International Date Line is considered east, and everything west of the Greenwich Meridian to the

International Date Line is considered west. That is why Israel is said to be in the "Middle East" and China is in the "Far East."

Longitude is the degree of the circle between 0° and 180°, either east or west of the Greenwich Meridian. As an example of how this is defined, the central portion of the United States is approximately 100° west, meaning that this area is 100° west of the Greenwich Meridian. China is approximately 100° east.

> 0° = Greenwich Meridian
> 180° East or West = International Date Line
> Central United States is approximately 100°W
> Central China is approximately 100°E

DEFINING A PRECISE LOCATION

Defining a location using the latitude and longitude is often called the lat-long. If you only used the degree of latitude or longitude to define a specific location, you would not be able to locate a particular spot very precisely. If you divide the entire northern hemisphere, from the equator to the North Pole, by 90° increments, each degree covers many miles.

In order to be more precise, each degree must be split into smaller increments. For example, a day is 24 hours, with each hour divided into 60 minutes, and each minute into 60 seconds; so that if you state the time as 2:12:32 PM, you have made that time very precise.

Latitude and longitude also use a 60-minute, 60-second system. Degrees of latitude and longitude are divided into increments of 60 minutes, and each minute is divided into 60 seconds. Each second of a degree equals 1/3600 of a degree. Lat-long is then two dimensions, written using the degree, minute, and second, and also stating north or south for latitude, or east or west for longitude.

A typical lat-long address looks like 40°39'15" N, 99°45'29" W. To define this location, it reads "40 degrees, 39 minutes, 15 seconds north" (of the Equator) and "99 degrees, 45 minutes, 29 seconds west" (of the Greenwich Meridian). This address would put you within only a very few yards of a precise location on the earth. You could get within inches by dividing the seconds into tenths or hundredths.

APPLYING LAT-LONG TO MAPS

On a map, you will notice grid lines running north and south, east and west. Some maps mark the degree of lat-long, but many do not. The grids on the map may not be a specific lat-long, but these lines will be parallel running true north and south, and east and west.

Using a Compass

A compass is nothing more than a magnetized piece of metal, sometimes suspended in a liquid, that rotates because of the earth's magnetic attraction until it aligns with the magnetic poles of the earth. The problem results because the magnetic poles of the earth are not at the same place that the true North and South Poles are located. The magnetic plates are actually a significant distance from the earth's true poles. The compass arrow points to magnetic north, not at the North Pole, and the lines on the map point to true north, the North Pole.

The difference between magnetic north and true north is called declination. The degree of declination varies considerably depending on your location. This might be only a few degrees — 7° to 15° in the central United States — up to many degrees in northern states or countries. The easiest method to determine declination in your area is to contact your local airport; pilots will know what the declination in a particular area is.

Once you have determined the degree of difference between the magnetic north that your compass is reading and true north on a map, you can use the compass to navigate accurately.

SILVA RANGER

The compass I use is a "Silva Ranger" type 15. It is a liquid filled compass that features an adjustment for declination, and has a clear base so you can see through it for map work. It has straight sides for drawing lines (plotting) on maps as well as several scales for calculation of distance, longitude, and latitude. It also has an inclinometer, used for measuring inclines, angles, and heights of objects. This compass also has a sighting mirror that can be used for a signal mirror. The adjustable ring is marked with all 360° bearing marks. It has a glow in the dark compass needle, and comes with an adjustable lanyard. This compass costs around $40 new, is very durable, and will last for many years. If I were to purchase another compass, it would have these features as a minimum. There are many other compasses made by many manufacturers of equal or better capability.

When using a compass you must always hold it flat so the needle will spin and settle on magnetic north. Make sure your compass is not influenced by any other magnetic fields. Radios, pagers, and cell phones can all contain magnets in the speakers, while vehicles, power lines, or other strong electric fields will also influence compass polarity.

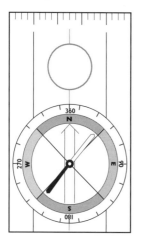

Around the face of most compasses there are numbers from 1 to 360. These are the 360° of the circle of direction. 0° and 360° are the same direction, north. 90° is due east, 180° is due south, and 270° is due west. These numbers are referred to as compass bearings.

My compass has an adjustment for declination, the difference between magnetic north and true north. At my particular location I set it for 7° east, meaning that magnetic deviation is 7° higher than true readings. If I did not have this adjustment, I would need to subtract 7° from every magnetic bearing to get true bearings. Map work is such an important part of compass work that every compass should have declination adjustments. A compass that does not have this feature can still be used very accurately, but it takes more time and creates another opportunity for errors.

PLOTTING POINT TO POINT

If you are at a known location and wish to go to another point, you can use your compass to guide you. This is especially helpful when traveling through heavy forest, at night, or anytime you cannot see landmarks. I have gone many miles in heavy, black timber and come to the desired location, within feet, by using a compass. My instincts would tell me that I was going in the wrong direction, but I trusted my compass and came out right on target. Had I followed my instincts, I would have been 90° wrong. It is easy to lose your sense of direction when you can't see landmarks, the sky, or other common reference points.

Scenario 1. You are located at Point A and wish to go to Point B. You can see Point B but will be going into dark heavy forest and will not be able to see Point B after you start moving.

Hold your compass flat, finding north. Now determine the degree of bearing that Point B is from you now. Since this process does not involve using maps, declination is not a factor. You do not need to make any adjustments since you will be able to navigate totally with magnetic bearings. Simply travel so that your degree of bearing remains the same. Once you are at

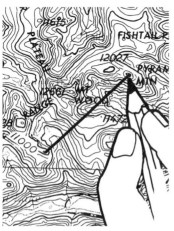

TAKING A COMPASS BEARING FROM A MAP:

1. *Draw a straight line on the map passing through your location and your desired destination.*

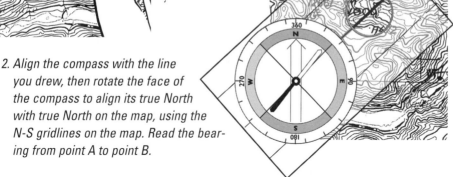

2. *Align the compass with the line you drew, then rotate the face of the compass to align its true North with true North on the map, using the N-S gridlines on the map. Read the bearing from point A to point B.*

3. *To use this bearing, you must compensate for magnetic declination. If the MN arrow on the map magnetic declination diagram is to the right of the true north line, subtract the MN value. If the arrow is to the left of the line, add the value. Then, standing on your location on the ground, set the compass so that 0° or North aligns with the magnetic north needle, read the magnetic bearing that you have determined by this procedure, and head off in the direction of this bearing to reach your destination.*

Remember that compass readings are affected by the presence of iron and steel objects. Be sure to look out for—and stay away from—pocket knives, belt buckles, trucks, electrical lines, and so forth when using a compass in the field.

Point B and want to go back to Point A, you can use the opposite bearing by adding 180°. (Remember the degrees only go up to 360° then start over, meaning 300° bearing plus 180° would be a new bearing of 120°.)

Scenario 2. You are located at Point A and desire to go to Point B. You cannot see Point B but know where it is on your map. Once you start moving you will be in heavy timber and unable to see landmarks.

Draw a line on your map from Point A to Point B. Lay your compass on the map with the edge of the compass aligned against the line you just drew. Rotate the face of the compass to align its north with true north on the map by using the grid lines on the map. Read the bearing from Point A to Point B. Since you are using true north on the map, you must adjust your magnetic bearing to compensate for declination. Once you have determined a magnetic bearing, you will be able to travel on that magnetic bearing to Point B. You will be able to return by adding 180°.

If you have problems plotting on a map remember that you can always turn the map so that north on the map is actually pointing north and take your bearings. If you are new at mapping or just want to check yourself, it is a good idea to do this anyway. If the map is turned to the actual direction, you will be able to see if things don't look right. If they do not, check your work.

Do not try to turn the map and plot magnetic bearings on the hood of a car, because the metal will prevent your compass from working correctly. If you are only using true bearings it won't be a problem.

TRIANGULATION

To determine a specific location you must be able to reference at least three dimensions. As stated before, you will use the ground surface as one dimension, making it necessary to determine your location by using only two additional dimensions or reference points.

You need to be able to identify two known landmarks or points of reference. These can be any distance from you, a few hundred feet to many miles away, as long as they are shown on the map you are using. These reference points can be any known location — a distant town, a lighted radio tower, a mountain, a highway intersection, an airport light beacon, or any known location you can see. If your reference points are not shown on the map you are using, then you may need to select a closer reference.

What you will be doing is taking a compass bearing from your location

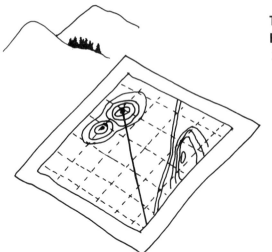

TO DETERMINE YOUR POSITION BY TRIANGULATION:

1. *Find a known landmark that appears on your map (a peak, tower, etc.). Point your compass toward the landmark to get a compass bearing, adjusting for declination. Lay your compass on the map, and using that bearing, draw a line across your map from the reference point.*

2. *Find a second landmark that also appears on your map. Again, point your compass toward the landmark to get a bearing, adjusting for declination. Draw a line through your map from the reference point using that bearing. Your location is where these two lines intersect.*

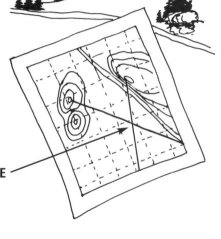

YOU ARE HERE

to each reference point. This will be a magnetic bearing so you need to adjust for declination and determine a true bearing. You will then transfer that true bearing onto your map by locating the reference point on the map, then drawing a line from that point on the true bearing you have determined. This is just a line across your map starting at the reference point and continuing indefinitely on the bearing you have determined.

Using the second reference point you will determine a second bearing, again adjusting for declination and transferring that line onto your map. The lines drawn will intersect at your location on the map. You can use as many reference points as necessary and draw as many lines as you want, but you will need a minimum of two bearings.

If you were lost and had phone or radio contact with another capable person who has maps, you could tell that person your bearings and have them plot the maps. If you ever do this, you must specify to that person whether you are providing magnetic or true bearings. This person can determine your location on the map and provide a compass bearing to follow.

There are a few things to remember when you are using triangulation to determine your location. The closer your reference points are to right angles from each other, the more accurate the point of intersection will be. If you choose two points that are only five degrees apart, the lines will intersect at a very narrow angle, which is difficult to decipher. If you choose reference points that are 180° apart the angle will be more like a straight line. Use reference points that are somewhere between 45° to 120° apart from each other so that you have a well-defined point of intersection on your maps. Multiple reference points will also help define your location.

Using a map and compass takes practice and experience. There are many types, styles, and features available, each having different application. Only first-hand experience will determine what works best for you.

SELECTING YOUR EQUIPMENT

Select a quality compass such as the "Silva Ranger" type. It should be on a lanyard, have the ability to adjust for declination, have a mirror, and sighting capability. It should also have a clear base for easier map work. Wear your compass on the lanyard (with your whistle) around your neck so that you will use it often. If you carry it in a pack, it is much more difficult to check, and you will not refer to it as often.

If you decide on a GPS receiver, learn how to use all the functions. Learn how to set waypoints (points along the way of a plotted course), and how to use every screen. The receivers are bulky and expensive, but very fun, accurate, and reliable. Carry a map of your area and compass as a backup system.

Select high-quality topographical maps that provide good detail and are easy to read, with coherent legends and useful information. The map must be durable and preferably waterproof. If it dissolves into little paper balls in your back pocket, it won't do you any good.

TRUST YOUR EQUIPMENT

Over the years I have seen many individuals who have gotten lost even with good mapping, compasses, and other systems. Many of these individuals insisted the equipment was wrong, the compass was off, or they just had the feeling the car was right over the hill.

On one hunting trip, I came across a couple of hunters standing in the middle of a trail during a heavy rainstorm. One hunter had a poor quality poncho and the other was just standing in the rain getting soaked. I carry a rain suit and a spare in my pack because I often have to support a second person during a rescue. The two hunters were obviously not well prepared; not in serious trouble yet, but heading in that direction. We were about a mile away from the road and in heavy black timber. In visiting with them, I could tell immediately that they had no idea what they were doing. I gave them the extra rain gear and showed them a large tree that they could sit under until the rain let up. They were much drier under the tree.

Carry your compass on a strong lanyard around your neck. If it is in your pack, you won't check it as often as you should.

Trust your compass!

Fir trees often make a good quick shelter because their needles shed the water away from the trunk of the tree. A person can stay much drier close to the trunk of the tree.

I gave the two hunters a quick lesson with my spare compass, with a bearing that would get them back to the highway. I told them that if they got lost to go the way the arrow pointed and they would come out somewhere on the highway. The highway traveled north and south to the east of our location then curved to the west south of our location. The hunters would definitely find it if they followed the compass setting.

We had agreed that they would leave my equipment in my pickup when they got out, since they had planned to be out much earlier than I would be. Later that night I returned to my pickup and realized they had not returned any of my gear. In fact, there was no sign that they had approached my vehicle at all. I figured they either ripped me off or had gotten lost, so I looked down the road for their vehicle. Sure enough it was still there.

I was loading up my gear when the two men stumbled out of the trees, dog-tired. They told me about getting lost about an hour after I had visited with them. They continued to be lost for about two hours before one of them decided to try the compass and bearing I had given them earlier.

They followed my instructions and discovered they had been walking 180 degrees in the wrong direction. They were sure the compass was wrong, but followed it anyway until they came out on the highway.

All the tools and all the toys will not do you any good if you don't trust them. Practice and experience will be the only way to develop that trust. Also, use good judgement. If you have a bad feeling about what you are getting into, then stop and rethink what you're doing. Trusting your judgement is just as important as trusting your equipment and will prevent many mistakes.

Fear of the Dark and Fear of Animals

It is surprising how many people are afraid of the dark. When the sun goes down and the lights go out, suddenly our surroundings look totally different and are somehow threatening. Imaginations run wild and subconsciously we feel the boogieman really does exist.

Fear of the dark is a common problem. Without light, we cannot rely on our sense of sight, so we pay more attention to the other senses including smell and hearing. Little noises that would be ignored with light become threatening and frightening as we try to determine what is making the noise. In a wilderness setting, this fear is compounded because of the unfamiliar surroundings and noises. One of the biggest fears people have of spending a night in the wilderness is a fear of animals.

I have camped in the open with no shelter and had coyote pups come up to within a couple of feet away, checking me out. I had heard them howling earlier and knew they were close, but went to bed. My fire had gone out, so that no longer scared them off. They came up behind me, took a couple of sniffs and left when I rolled over. That might unnerve some people, but it was an incredible experience.

Once on a night search I walked up on a black bear that could not get away from me fast enough. It was only about twenty yards away and crashing through the bushes to leave. We heard it circle around us in the darkness and go right back to its area when we left. This was its turf, and we were the ones who were being invasive.

Part of dealing with a fear of the dark or a fear of wildlife is to realize that most animals are more afraid of you than you are of them. Animals don't want problems; they are just checking out who is passing through their home. Very seldom will you find or hear about an aggressive or threatening animal. It rarely happens, but when it does, it gets so much publicity that people think it happens all the time. The public perception is that you will surely be eaten by some bear, wolf, or big cat if you spend a night in the wilderness. This is simply not true.

Part of dealing with a fear of the dark or a fear of wildlife is to realize that most animals are more afraid of you than you are of them.

Most wildlife will leave an area well before you arrive (we tend to be noisy creatures), unless it is cornered, has young in the area, or feels threatened for some other reason. Once camped, a campfire will keep most animals away.

Food is one thing that will attract some animals, especially raccoons, opossum, and bears. Use common sense when storing food. If you keep food close to your body, you just might be baiting them to your location. If you try to take it away from them, you might cause a confrontation. Store food or anything else that might attract animals away from you if you're nervous about an encounter.

There are certain animals that are known for not having a fear of man and can be quite territorial. Animals such as the bull moose, grizzly bear, buffalo, or any species with young could become protective and aggressive. Regardless, animals are not a realistic threat in the wilderness. Be rational about your fears, not paranoid or imaginative. Maintain a positive mental attitude about the darkness and about the creatures around you.

7

Detectability

I n the wilderness, objects are not as detectable as you may think. You would think that something as large as a crashed airplane would be very noticeable. However, they are often very difficult to spot. It seems that most planes are white with white wings—when they crash in white snow they are almost invisible. I wish the FAA would require the topside of airplane wings to be painted fluorescent orange or some other bright color.

In searching for downed aircraft, we look for damage to the landscape that was caused when the plane went down. Broken trees, burned areas, and debris blowing around are often much more noticeable than the actual wreckage.

One plane crash we were searching for was in western Routt County Colorado. It was a fall day, the leaves were still on the trees, and everything was in full foliage. We had a report of an ELT (emergency location transmitter) signal in the area and a report of a missing private plane. We initiated an intensive ground search; CAP (Civil Air Patrol) was involved, flying grid search patterns.

It was midmorning when one of the CAP planes spotted the wreckage. Our command post was notified of the sighting. Another searcher and I were in the area on four-wheelers. Our command post would give us the coordinates of the crash site as soon as they could determine our exact location. The pilot was unable to spot us, even though we were on four-wheelers and out in the open. We decided to use signal mirrors to flash the pilot of the plane so he could determine our exact location. He was able to detect the flash immediately.

We were given a compass bearing and approximate distance to the crash. We proceeded in that direction, but could not spot the wreckage. The ELT signal had ended many hours earlier, so we were relying only on the visual sighting by the pilot.

We were told we were at the location, but we found no wreckage, so we contacted the command post and told them to have the pilot fly over the wreckage and dip his wing when he was right over it. The pilot was right over our heads when he dipped his wing, but we still saw nothing. The process was repeated with the same results.

We started sweeping the area and found the wreckage only 150 feet from where we were standing. The plane had crashed into the tall grass and was nearly invisible from the ground. The fuselage had burned, but the fire had been confined to a very small area. This plane had hit the ground without breaking any trees, one sign we look for. In this case, all three occupants had died on impact.

If a crashed plane can be so difficult to see, a lone human being can be nearly impossible, especially in heavy cover. Therefore, you must learn what you can do to be more easily detected in a rescue situation.

Clothing

Make yourself as visible as possible. If you are a hunter and you are wearing camouflage clothing, reverse the outfit so that the hunter orange is showing. If you do not have hunter orange clothing, wear the lightest or brightest piece of clothing you have. If you are stranded in snow, put on clothing that will contrast with the snow. When purchasing jackets and hats, think about their visibility. Bright red, yellow, and orange are all easier to detect than neutral colors.

Fire

Build a fire no matter what time of year it is and no matter how warm you might be. Fire is as crucial for detectability as it is for providing warmth in cold weather. Smoke rising out of the trees is very unnatural and can be spotted at great distances. If the weather is calm you can fill an entire valley with smoke. If searchers can narrow a search down to a single valley, the smoke will greatly reduce the search area. Putting green pine boughs or other green vegetation on the fire generates a column of smoke. During the day, occasionally throw green pine boughs or other green vegetation on the fire to generate a column of smoke. If a breeze is blowing and an experienced searcher gets a whiff of smoke, he will check wind direction and follow the clue. Smoke is very easily spotted in most cases.

Smoke is not visible at night, but the light from a campfire is very noticeable, either directly or from the light reflected on trees and surroundings. Maintain your fire throughout the night. Do not assume a search ends with darkness. Search groups often send up aircraft or go to vantage points at night to try and spot a campfire. If you hear aircraft in your area, stoke up your fire as quickly as possible. It takes preparation to be able to flare up your fire at a moment's notice, so have materials ready to go. Use dry pine tree branches, dry pine needles, dried weeds, or other man-made materials that ignite quickly and burn bright.

Sound for Detection

Noise can be a very good means of signaling. Sound is directional, meaning that searchers may hear something from a distance and be able to pinpoint its location.

Gunshot. Typically three rapid gunshots is a signal of distress. However, it might also mean that a hunter needs some practice at the range. It never fails that you will be searching for a lost hunter and hear three rapid shots. The searcher responds with three rapid shots, but the lost person has only two shells left. If you are lost and shooting three shots in the air means you will run out of ammo quickly, use your bullets conservatively.

Fire your rounds when it will do the most good. Searchers will often fire three rounds in the area in an effort to get a response. The searchers, usually several teams, contact each other by radio and advise when a particular team will be firing the rounds. All teams will then sit quietly, listening for a response. This is a good time to use your three rounds. It is also a good idea to fire your three rounds at night, since legal hunting usually ends at sunset. Rounds fired at night are very distinct.

Many hunters will carry a small caliber, second sidearm such as a .22-caliber pistol. The sound from a .22-caliber pistol is distinctly different than that of a high-powered rifle. Extra ammo for the smaller caliber sidearm is also much easier to carry.

Whistles. Every person going into any backcountry setting should carry a plastic, ball-type whistle on a lanyard hanging around their neck. Whistles are easy to blow for long periods of time and the sound can be heard for miles. Ball-type whistles make a vibrating sound that is very distinct from animal sounds. Whistles are also very inexpensive. The whistle should be a quality, plastic type (metal ones stick to your lips in cold weather). Select a whistle that can hold up in your pack and a lanyard that will keep it on your neck.

Whistles and Children. Children, especially small children, should be taught how to use a whistle and how to wear one. When you go camping, hiking, or any place that your child might wander off, give them a whistle with instructions before you leave the car. Make it special for them as a means to call for help if they get into any type of trouble. Advise them of how important it is for them to keep it with them at all times, day and night. Advise them that it is only to be used if they get lost, scared, injured or need help for any reason. Tell them that if they hear you blow a whistle they should blow their whistle back as a response.

Kids feel special and proud wearing a whistle. They will be dying to blow it, so once in awhile get everyone together and have a few whistle blowing sessions. Give every child who can walk a whistle on a lanyard around their neck.

Screaming or Shouting. Verbal noises take a lot of physical effort and should be used very conservatively. If you have ever tried screaming or shouting for any length of time, you know that it takes a lot of physical energy. You will soon be hoarse and perhaps unable to talk. I do not recommend screaming or shouting for help unless you know that help is very close. If you hear searchers, then you should attempt verbal contact.

Signal Mirrors

When selecting gear, include a glass signal mirror. There are several types on the market including some that have sights for pointing accurately. A glass signal mirror can be seen for many miles if used correctly.

On one occasion, I was in a helicopter and was signaled by a searcher on a mountain nearly seven miles away. It was a clear, bright day and as brilliant as that reflection was, I could have seen it from a much greater distance.

Select a glass mirror, not a metal or plastic one. Even though plastic and glass might look similar up close, there is a tremendous difference in performance at a distance. Glass mirrors require more care in a pack, but the extra performance is worth the effort.

Some compasses such as the Silva Ranger style have a signal mirror as part of the plastic case. This is a plastic mirror but performs well and is easy to pack.

SIGHTING MIRRORS

Sighting mirrors (signal mirrors with a sight) are highly recommended. They cost more, but can very accurately put a spot of sunlight on a target miles away. A sighting mirror looks like a normal mirror but has a clear spot in the center. To use, hold the mirror in one hand and reflect the sunlight from the mirror onto your other hand. While maintaining the sun's reflection on your free hand, bring the mirror up to your eye and see a bright spot of light in the sighting hole. Holding the mirror close to your eye, tilt and turn the mirror until you cover the target with the light spot.

The disadvantage of this type of mirror is that the light spot can be very bright and hard on your eyes with extended use. This mirror will also need to be packed carefully so it does not break. The benefits far outweigh any disadvantages, however.

SIGHTING A NORMAL MIRROR

Sighting a regular mirror at a target is not as easy as you might think. When sitting in your living room, use a mirror to shine sunlight at various points in the room. This is easy because you have walls and other objects to reference where the light is shining, and then you can tilt and turn the mirror to hit your target.

When you go outside, it becomes much more difficult because you lose your reference points. You might be able to reflect a spot of light on nearby trees or buildings, but you will notice it becomes difficult to see the light spot on moving branches or distant buildings. Additionally, try to shine it on the top of a nearby telephone pole or any other object where the sky is the background. This is very difficult because you have little or no reference points. If you are lost and trying to reflect light on an aircraft a distance away, the problem becomes even more difficult because the aircraft has no reflective background.

To sight a regular mirror, hold the mirror directly in front of, and directly under, your eye. You should be just peeking over the top edge. Extend your other arm and point your fingertips up; shine the sunlight on the tips of your fingers. You should now have the mirror tight against your face, and the light spot barely shining on the fingertips of your extended arm. You now have two reference points — your face and your fingertips — that you can align over your target. Move your mirror, head, and arm as a single unit until you are pointing at the target, then move that spot up and down, back and forth over the target. Practice this technique before you are in an emergency situation.

Signal mirrors, if used correctly, can be annoying or even blinding to a pilot because the light is very intense. If you are annoying them, you at least have their attention. Once you are sure a pilot has spotted you, stop signalling him or her with the mirror.

Use a mirror as long as you have light available. The spotters might be looking the other direction for an extended period of time and not see you right away. Search planes will commonly fly grid patterns over a specific area, concentrating their attention in that grid. They might not notice your light until they fly that particular grid.

I recommend flashing any aircraft that you see in the area including commercial airlines. Commercial flights might not be participating in any search activity, but they often monitor radio traffic from other aircraft and could be aware of the search. If they are aware of the search and see the flashing light, they may relay that location to the search planes or other local authorities. I have been assisted on several searches by commercial aircraft. The searches were for lost aircraft. The commercial pilots, aware of the search activity, detected E.L.T. information and relayed it to the search planes flying below.

Artificial Lights

Artificial lights are very effective detection devices. Flashlights, strobe lights, and other lights can be spotted at night very easily from great distances. Lights flashing on trees or shining on other objects are very noticeable. Shining a beam of light into the sky at night often creates an airport beacon effect.

The disadvantage of artificial lights is the battery requirement. If you waste your batteries shining your light up in the sky, you won't have anything left when you need it. With the exception of strobes at night, I would only use the lights around camp as needed.

Strobe Lights. Strobe lights are highly recommended to carry in a pack. Strobes are small, inexpensive and easily detectable. They operate for long periods of time on a single battery, and the brilliant white light produced can be seen for many miles. Strobes can also be used to illuminate your camp or trail as you walk. Your eyes will adjust to operating by the flash and you will be able to navigate through the darkness. If you're moving, put the strobe high on your body, on your hat if possible. If you are camping, place the strobe on a highpoint nearby so it can be seen from the widest possible angle.

Signal mirrors, if used correctly, can be annoying or even blinding to a pilot because the light is very intense. Once you are sure a pilot has spotted you, stop signalling him or her with the mirror.

Flashlights and Headlamps. Flashlights and headlamps should be a basic part of your pack. There are many types of flashlights and headlamps that have different battery requirements. Select your equipment so that all items use the same battery size, if possible, so that you will need fewer spares. With the exception of my strobe light, I prefer to use lights that require AA batteries. The batteries are small and yet deliver good light.

Headlamps are great flashlights because they leave your hands free. If you need to work on any activity requiring your hands you will appreciate the hands-free feature. A small Maglight or Streamline-type of flashlight does a good job and can be held in your mouth if necessary. This type of flashlight is very durable, water resistant, and has an adjustable beam.

Batteries have a tendency to run out when you need them the most. If you don't believe that, then allow a child to play with your flashlight. It will work all day and night for them; when you have a power failure and really need it, the light turns yellow and goes out. If your batteries go dead, try letting them sit for a while or warm them up; often you can sneak a little more life out of them.

Use your resources conservatively. If you are traveling at night, flash your light every once in a while to check reference points, but try keeping it off as much as possible. Let your eyes adjust to the darkness and use your campfire for a nightlight. Fires give off enough light to comfort you and will save your other resources.

Glow Sticks. Glow sticks are plastic tubes that contain two chemicals, one inside a glass vial, that react and put off light. To activate, you bend the glow stick and break the internal vial and start the chemical reaction. The sticks do not give off enough light to be practical for navigation or sight, but they do make a person very detectable. These can be attached to clothing, hats, wrists, etc., or hung up around camp to attract attention.

I personally have not used glow sticks except on a couple of searches where we were walking grids at night. We used them to keep track of each other. They do work well but can only be seen for a limited distance.

One funny story that involved glow sticks was told to me by a dog handler in Colorado. On a search, a dog was outfitted with a special Search and Rescue vest for identification and protection. The vest also had loops to attach six glow sticks so the handlers could keep track of the dog at night. You will have to imagine what the dog must have looked like in the dark with six green glowing lights all over its body.

The lost man was already terrified from being lost, but became even more terrified when he heard something approaching that was obviously not human, hot on his trail, busting through the grass and bushes. The next thing he saw was the green, glowing creature coming after him no matter where he went or how well he hid. When it was all over, he stated that he thought he was going to be the next victim of an alien abduction.

Infrared Detectability

Technology in the field of search and rescue has greatly improved over the years. Infrared systems are becoming more affordable for smaller agencies. The military will also often assist civilian searches as part of their practice and training.

FLIR technology uses infrared light to detect anything that produces heat. Campfires, body heat, heat on objects from sunlight during the day, or any temperature differences will make objects visible in total darkness. This equipment is so sensitive that it can detect warm spots on the ground where an animal has recently lain.

If you see aircraft searching the area, even if quite high, make yourself visible. Aircraft with infrared detection devices might be flying grid patterns and filming the area for review, or monitoring the area in actual time. Though infrared can see your heat picture through trees, you will be more visible if you move into a clearing.

Be Creative

In order to become more detectable, it often takes creativity. Consider using any object that would look out of place and catch someone's attention. A trash bag on a branch makes a flag; the word "HELP" or "SOS" stamped out in the snow or spelled out with pine boughs on white snow is very noticeable. If you must continue moving, tie bits of torn cloth or paper onto trees to mark your direction. Do whatever you can to stand out in your environment.

8
Surviving in Your Vehicle

Getting into trouble is not difficult for me at all; I have done it on many occasions. One incident happened a few years ago in central Wyoming. My family and I had moved away from Colorado about a year earlier. Our good friends lived in Steamboat Springs, Colorado, and offered to take one of my daughters on their vacation to Florida to keep their own daughter amused.

My family had already planned a trip to Yellowstone, Wyoming, for a brief vacation. We decided that I would drive to Steamboat Springs with my daughter, spend a few days after there house-sitting for our friends, then travel to Yellowstone and meet the rest of my family, who would be driving there from Nebraska. We planned to spend a few days at Yellowstone, then my wife would travel back home while I returned to Steamboat Springs to house-sit for an additional week.

It's an 8-hour drive between Steamboat Springs and Yellowstone. I didn't tell anyone in Steamboat that I would be in town because I wanted to relax and drop in on friends at my leisure. Everything went according to plan. I met my family in Yellowstone, had a good time, and then we separated.

I am noted for driving "disposable vehicles," "old beaters," "junk," or whatever you want to call them. I referred to my car as the "Nissan OPUS" (Old Piece Uh Something) model. I get a kick out of paying $200 for a car and seeing how much life I can choke out of it. Travel in these vehicles is an adventure in itself.

Wyoming is one of the most sparsely populated areas in the country. In certain areas, everything looks the same — flat, sagebrush, a few rocks, a few hills, the wind always blowing, and a few cattle or sheep.

On the return trip to Steamboat, I chose not to use the road map because I had already traveled this road on my way to Yellowstone. Just south of Riverton, Wyoming, I needed to take an oiled road marked 135 south, which would come out on State Hwy 287. By mistake, I took a road marked 136 and did not realize it until I had traveled 40 miles and the asphalt ended and turned into gravel. A heavy rain had just passed through the area and left the roads extremely muddy. I should have turned around and driven the 40 miles back to Riverton, but instead decided to try and drive the gravel road and pick my way down to Jeffrey City on the back roads.

I traveled south for about 20 miles until the gravel road was barricaded by some mining operation with signs to keep out of the area. I knew I couldn't be that many miles from the highway I needed be on and found a four wheel-drive road that was heading in the general direction I needed to go. I should have turned around and driven the 60 miles back to Riverton.

I followed the four-wheel drive road until it faded into the sagebrush, and soon I was just driving around without a road of any kind, completely lost, in a car that was a piece of junk, low on fuel, and with bad tires. I had driven around enough that now I couldn't find the road that I had driven in on.

At this point, the reality started to set in. I was out in the middle of Wyoming, lost, and driving through the sagebrush. My family wouldn't miss me because they were traveling home through the Black Hills thinking that I was in Steamboat Springs. My wife wouldn't think it was odd if I didn't answer the phone that night, figuring I was probably just visiting someone. Nobody in Steamboat Springs knew I was supposed to be in town, so no one there would realize that I was overdue. I also realized that when someone did miss me, the search area would be not only the entire length of Wyoming, but I was 60 miles off course, in the middle of nowhere.

I started getting into my "survival mode." I made mental notes of where I was seeing water, or vegetation that indicated water. I was still driving and looking for anything that looked like a landmark, a road, or a vantage point. I was assessing what supplies I had along and started making long term plans. I thought about how I could make myself more detectable, but wasn't sure anyone was around to notice. I thought about using one of the mirrors in the car to flash an aircraft, vehicle, or anything else that might come along.

I continued driving through the brush and rocks and finally spotted an old roadbed in the distance. I picked my way through the sagebrush, rocks, and dried creek beds, driving as carefully as I could to protect my tires and keep from getting stuck or high centered. Finally, I reached the old roadbed and drove west, figuring it would either end up on highway 287 or intersect route 135. The old roadbed wasn't too bad; it was much easier to travel over and at least I was following something.

I traveled for two miles on this road when I came upon a little concrete marker that stated "Historical Marker, Oregon Trail." I actually laughed out loud when I realized I was driving a 1981 Nissan OPUS with bald tires down the Oregon Trail. I knew my family and friends would never believe this one, but I didn't have the camera. My thoughts were beginning to focus on whether I was breaking some federal law by damaging a historical area or something. Then it hit me — what could be more detectable than some "bonehead" driving an old junker down the Oregon Trail. If law enforcement was going to come after me, at least someone would tell me how to get out of there.

I drove the Oregon Trail for another eight miles and eventually spotted the highway to the south. I found a place to cross a creek bed and then drove into a hay meadow, followed the fence lines to a gate, and came out on the highway. My mistakes had cost me quite a bit of time and made me a little nervous, but I did get to see the Oregon Trail.

The Prepared Motorist

All of the information covered so far has been intended for the person who is lost in the outdoors. However, the odds of being stranded in a vehicle are much more likely than being stranded in a wilderness setting. Most drivers are completely unprepared. Traveling on busy highways does not insure that you will not be stranded for hours waiting for someone to stop. Many travelers have so much faith in their vehicles — the car's heater, battery, their cell phone, or other mechanical devices — that they travel in very cold weather and don't even carry a warm coat; they plan to be in the car at all times.

I once encountered a stranded motorist on a remote stretch of highway between Denver and Steamboat Springs. My wife and I were coming back from Denver on a very cold winter day and noticed a car on the side of the road with a couple inside. The windows were iced up and the vehicle had been sitting there for some time. We stopped to see if they needed help and they begged for a ride. They had been sitting for hours and been passed by several vehicles. We loaded them into our vehicle and took them to town.

There are many reasons a vehicle can stop running, leaving you stranded. If the engine dies, you will have no engine heat, which means you have no heater and the car will get cold quickly. If you are stranded because of a flat tire and can still run the engine, you run the risk of carbon monoxide (CO) poisoning. People die every year because they did not understand that a vehicle is not airtight. To prove this point, if you drive near a dead skunk in the road, the smell hits you almost instantly. The ease in which air circulates odors into your vehicle shows that deadly gasses circulate as easily. It takes only a small hole in the exhaust system, a lack of air movement, or the right wind current to bring carbon monoxide into your vehicle. I do not recommend using a vehicle heater for warmth for any extended period of time. If you do use your car heater, never go to sleep, and pay attention to any headaches, a warning symptom of CO poisoning. Turn off your engine if you need to sleep, or if you have a headache.

The need to minimize the chance of breaking down is very important. There are many things you can do to prepare for the possibility of being stranded.

CHANGING A TIRE

Everyone who drives should know how to change a flat tire, including women and teenagers. While safely in your driveway, get the jack out, read the instructions, and discover where on your car it goes (on all four tire areas) to jack up the car. Practice jacking up the car at least once.

Loosening the lugnuts is often the most difficult part of changing a tire, but this is easily accomplished if you start to loosen them before you jack up the car. When the car is still on the ground, put the tire wrench on one of the lugnuts and turn the wrench until you feel the lugnut loosen. If you need to apply more force to loosen the nuts, try using the jack handle to add leverage to the lug wrench, or stomp on the wrench with your foot. Continue to loosen all four or six of the lugnuts. Then jack up the car. When you loosen the lugnuts in this way, the weight and strength of your leg breaks the seal, and the weight of the car keeps the tire steady. If you raise the car first, the tire will turn as you try to break the lugnut seal, and you will have to rely only on arm strength.

Once you have placed the spare tire on the car, tighten the lugnuts in the same way. While the car is still up in the air, hand-tighten each of the lugnuts. When you jack the car back down, tighten the lugnuts securely.

There are several brands of aerosol tire inflaters that will inflate your tire enough to limp back to a service station. While these products work well on very small punctures, they will not work on larger holes, blowouts, or cuts. If you purchase this type of tire inflater, make sure the can is large enough to inflate your tire size. **Warning:** If you use an aerosol tire inflater, advise the person making the tire repair. Many brands use butane, propane, or other highly-explosive gases as propellents, that could be accidentally ignited by a repair person.

MAINTAINING YOUR VEHICLE

Proper maintenance will not guarantee that you will never be stranded, but it will help. During the winter, keep your gas tank full. Fill it up at the one-half mark and make a habit of never letting it get below that level. Water in gas can freeze in the gas lines and filters, preventing gas from reaching the engine. Water gets into fuel lines from condensation of water vapor within the gas tank. If the tank is kept full, there is less moist air in the tank.

There are several gas additives on the market that remove water from the fuel system. During cold winter months, add these to your fuel tank once in a while, and keep an unopened container of it in your trunk.

You should know how to check and fill all fluids in a vehicle, which include oil, radiator, brake, window washer, transmission, and power steering fluids. Use common sense. If you are about to take off across the desert regions of Arizona or Nevada, check the water level in the radiator and top it off. Carry an extra jug or two of water just for the engine. Similarly, check the oil more often in both extreme hot and extreme cold temperatures. Extreme temperatures in either direction put a lot of wear on a vehicle's fluids. If you are traveling for any distance, check them regularly.

Vehicle Survival Kit

Put together a survival kit that is appropriate for the environment you will be passing through. If you are traveling through a desert area, drinking water and extra water for the car's engine are the most important items, but you may also want additional clothing for the colder temperatures after dark, a few fire starters, and perhaps sunscreen, a hat, a little bit of food, etc. If you are going through snowy or icy conditions, good snow boots, a hat, warm jacket, insulated gloves or mittens, and a scarf are crucial. If you need to walk to get help, even for a short distance, you will need this gear as a minimum. Gloves are necessary if you need to change a tire or work on the engine. The following suggestions are additional items for traveling in cold weather conditions. These extra items can be stored in the car's trunk.

Sleeping Bag. A sleeping bag in the trunk is worth its weight in gold if you have to stay put for any length of time. It can be cozy for one person or opened up and used as a quilt for more than one. The more people in a vehicle the more body heat you will have. A sleeping bag can be stored in a garbage bag to keep it from getting dusty and dirty in the trunk of the car.

Candles. Candles do emit a little heat, but are not really much use for staying warm. They do make good light, though, which makes you much more detectable. The flickering light from a single candle in a vehicle, even with the windows iced up, will indicate to a passerby that someone is still in the vehicle. Carbon monoxide poisoning is highly unlikely from a candle flame.

Lighter. A candle will not work if you can't light it, so pack some sort of cigarette lighter or matches in your vehicle. The vehicle cigarette lighter will work if you can light a piece of paper and then light your candle. Do not depend on this lighter, though, because if your battery is dead, it won't work.

Kitty Litter. No, not for that. Kitty litter makes an excellent traction sand if you get stuck on ice and need a little more traction. Throw it under the spinning tires. The extra weight in the trunk also helps with traction.

Toilet Paper. Yes, for that. If you've got to go, you might as well be civilized about it. You might have to squat in the grass or snow next to your car along the highway, but at least you'll be more comfortable.

ITEMS TO KEEP IN YOUR CAR:

- [ ] *Tire jack and spare, jumper cables*
- [ ] *Flares*
- [ ] *Water for drinking and car's radiator*
- [ ] *Food, such as energy bar, candy bar, or trail mix*

In cold weather/mountains:

- [ ] *Warm clothes, including boots, coat, warm gloves, hat and scarf.*
- [ ] *Sleeping bag*
- [ ] *Candles*
- [ ] *Lighter and matches*
- [ ] *Kitty litter*
- [ ] *Toilet paper*
- [ ] *Emergency heater such as the Papa Bear heater*

Papa Bear Heater. The Papa Bear heater is named after Papa Bear Whitmore, a well-known survival instructor in Colorado. He "invented" this emergency vehicle heater which works very well. You will need an empty one-pound coffee can with the plastic lid, a roll of toilet paper, and two bottles of rubbing alcohol. Roll the toilet paper roll back and forth in your palms to loosen the cardboard core. Gently pull the core out without disturbing the paper, if possible. Compress the toilet paper and slide it into the coffee can. Pour one bottle of rubbing alcohol into the can and allow the toilet paper to soak it up. Hold the can in your hand and light the top with a lighter. Alcohol burns exceptionally clean and will not produce carbon monoxide. The flame is almost invisible so you must be careful; this is one reason you need to hold the can in your hand. To light the can, hold the flame of the lighter just barely over the edge of the can, as alcohol could flash and singe your hand.

This is a very safe heater if used properly. The only thing that burns is the alcohol vapor that evaporates from the toilet paper. If you notice the toilet paper starting to turn brown on the top edges, you are running out of alcohol and need to add more. Extinguish the flame before pouring in more alcohol.

You should not use this heater 100 percent of the time. Like any other resource, you must use it conservatively, making it last until help arrives. Warm your vehicle to a point you can tolerate, and then blow the heater out with one large breath. Once the rim of the can is cool, place the plastic lid back on to prevent the evaporation of the remaining alcohol.

I have used this heater for several applications, including a vehicle heater. It does an excellent job, and will last a surprising length of time. If used conservatively, two small bottles of rubbing alcohol will last forty-eight hours. Do not forget your lighter so you can start the fire.

To pack the heater, place the toilet paper in the coffee can, leaving it dry. Place a lighter on top of the toilet paper, put the plastic lid on, and tape the lid down. Then tape two *unopened* bottles of alcohol to the outside of the can and store it in the trunk. If you pour the alcohol into the can before you store it, the alcohol will be dried out when you need it.

CELL PHONES

Cell phones are great in emergencies and do give an extra level of insurance. However, they are not fail-proof.

If your survival plan is to simply call AAA on your cell phone and let them take care of any vehicle problems, you could find yourself in trouble. Cell phones do not always work when you need them. They can be damaged in a crash, the batteries can die, or the signal may be out of range. If you are in hills or a low area, you might have a weak or non-existent signal.

The proper antenna on your cell phone makes a big difference on its effective range. A hand-held phone has a fraction of the signal strength as that of bag phones. External antennas also have a much better range. Many hand-held phones come with adapters so that they can be used with an external antenna. If your cell phone has this capability, you should make the extra investment. Cell phones are like any other radio and have a much better range with a higher antenna. Raising the antenna a few inches can make a considerable difference. If you have a signal problem inside your car, move outside of the vehicle. If it is still bad, move to a higher location; even standing on your vehicle can make a difference.

Know Your Location

If your cell phone does work, could you tell someone where you are? If you are in a strange area, you will probably have a difficult time describing any landmarks. Most people do not keep track of highway mile markers while traveling. Getting in the habit of watching mile markers could make a significant response time difference. The next time you're going down the highway, play a little game and ask yourself, "how would I tell a 911 dispatcher this exact location if I needed help?"

Surprisingly, most of us get into such a routine while we are traveling that we often do not keep track of the towns we pass through, let alone the mile markers. If suddenly you were in need of help, knowing the name of the last town you passed would be essential. Human nature is to daydream along the route and only switch our brains back on when we get close to our destination. You need to train yourself into the habit of keeping track of where you are at all times. Make a game of it with your kids or surprise other adults with the question, "If the car ahead of us rolled over, what would you tell a 911 dispatcher about the location?" It can be an amusing little game and will encourage them to think at the same time. Keep in mind that when you are pretending, you will have the advantage of looking at the next mile marker. If it were a real emergency, you would not be moving and have that option.

Staying with the Vehicle or Seeking Help

Your vehicle is the best shelter you could possibly hope for. It is very detectable unless it gets covered by snow or goes off the road and cannot be seen. Think seriously before leaving that shelter. There have been cases of hard, driving blizzards in which individuals became turned around and lost trying to get from the front of their car to the trunk. Be careful and use common sense.

If you see lights from a residence, be careful you're not deceived by distance. At night, lights may look closer than they actually are and can be many miles away. Unless you are exceptionally well-dressed, have a survival pack, and know how to use its contents, in adverse weather, you should stay with your vehicle.

9

Venturing Out:
Clothing, Footwear, Plans, and Packs

O ne beautiful late winter day a young, athletic couple decided to go cross-country skiing for a few hours. They were vacationing together, alone, with no real plans, and staying in one of the condos to enjoy the area. They had stopped at a local ski shop, picked up a ski trail map, and decided, "spur of the moment," to take a little trip into the backcountry. It was already mid-morning, but they planned to ski a marked cross-country ski trail that was moderately difficult, but would have them back at the road by four PM, nearly two hours before dark. These trails are marked by little blue diamonds nailed to the trees or a pole every several hundred yards, not necessarily visible from one to the other. Normally, the tracks of other skiers would make the trail quite obvious. The trail went into the National Forest for several miles then looped back to its starting point.

The young couple was not familiar with the area, as they were vacationing from the east. They didn't realize that it is not unusual in the Rockies for temperatures to drop from well above freezing during the day to -20°F at night. They were, however, experienced skiers and would have no problem maneuvering at a good pace down the trails.

This was a hastily-planned, impulsive trip, and they traveled lightly. In fact, all they had taken along was a bota full of wine, a little cheese, and the trail map. It was a beautiful, warm day in the mid-40s to the low 50s, so this should have been all they needed, right? So off they went.

The couple was wearing "fashionable" clothing: tight spandex skiwear that looked good on the ski slopes. The woman wore a hat, but the man did not. They had gloves, but otherwise were dressed for the current, very pleasant temperatures and sunshine. Since they were confident, experienced skiers, their intent was that they would just ski back out to the road if the weather changed. How long could that take?

The area had received a heavy snowfall with blowing winds the previous night. The snow had filled areas of the ski trail with fresh snow, drifting in some areas quite deeply. The warm temperatures of the day had settled the snow pack quickly. The area near the highway where the couple started was somewhat protected, leaving the trail visible and the new, untracked snow, was very tempting.

The couple started on the ski trail around noon. They followed the trail, admiring the beauty of the area, with fresh snow adorning the trees; naturally they were caught up in the experience. The first couple of miles went very well. They traveled over a few drifts, occasionally seeing the older cross-country tracks for reference. They both developed an "eye" for spotting the little blue diamonds that marked the trail.

Earlier that week, Search and Rescue had been called for a lost skier in the same general area. On this very trail, a skier had made a mistake and skied into the wrong drainage, which had taken him a great distance off the trail. He had been rescued safely, but he had gone several miles off the intended route before he was found.

The couple had been referencing whatever visible track they could spot as well as the blue diamonds, but they followed the track of the previously lost skier into the wrong drainage. This was a costly mistake, both in time and effort because this was a very steep drainage that was difficult to ski out of. Once you started over the edge, you would usually be committed to go to the bottom to travel out because backtracking up the slope was so difficult.

The couple soon noticed that they were not seeing the blue diamond trail markers. Realizing that they were getting into trouble, they decided to try a different direction. They knew they needed to go back and find the trail.

The couple struggled to get back on the rim of the drainage, sidestepping on their skies up the side of the hill. Once on top of the rim, they headed in a direction they both felt would intercept their old track. In fact, they had chosen a direction that ran parallel to their ski track — they would never cross their old track.

It got dark around 5:30 to 6 PM, and they had lost several hours of precious daylight. They were staying in a condo alone, so no one would miss them and no one would be looking for them. Panic began to set in as they watched the darkness fall and felt the temperatures drop.

It seemed to be a miracle, but within only a few minutes of total darkness the couple spotted a very small wooden building in the distance, sticking out of the snow. It was a 6' x 6', insulated but unheated wooden shack that is used as a weather monitoring station during parts of the year. They needed to dig the door out, which was down in about five feet of snow. The hasp and lock were no problem for the panicked couple; they pried it off using a ski.

It was then dark, the temperatures dropped to subzero, the snows started, and the wind was blowing. The couple had protection from the elements, but they still had no lights, no candles, and no heat. They had accepted the fact that they would be spending at least this night in the shed. For warmth, they pulled fiberglass insulation from the walls and wrapped themselves together, sharing body heat.

. . . the skiers made mistakes before they ever took off. They were in a new area and were over-confident about their abilities. They didn't leave word with anyone about their plans.

Early the next morning, the Colorado Department of Roads reported that a vehicle had been parked at the trailhead over night. People don't park cars along the highway, 15 miles from town in the winter. This report was investigated as a possible lost skier.

Sheriff's deputies gained entry to the vehicle and were able to determine in which condo the couple should have been staying. We interviewed the management company and found that the couple had not spent the night in their unit. We were also able to visit with the receptionist who had checked them in, and learned other details about the couple. This receptionist had recommended a couple of ski shops and had talked with them about the cross-country skiing in the area.

Based on the vehicle being at the trailhead and the couple's interest in cross-country skiing, we launched a ground search of the area. It was approximately 10 AM when the snowmobiles went into the ski area to see what they could find.

The couple had stayed very warm and safe through the night. The shed, fiberglass insulation, and their body heat had saved their lives and they knew it. The night had been miserable because of the itch from the fiberglass, but they were safe and alive.

The weather had cleared and it was a bright, warm day. Blowing snow had filled their tracks during the night. The couple now had a real lack of confidence and with the new snow and different lighting, everything took on a new appearance. The couple felt hopelessly lost. They were reluctant to leave their shelter, knowing that the coming night could be as bad as the previous one. A decision had to be made. Should they gamble and leave the shelter, chancing they would find the road before night, or should they stay at the shelter and face another cold, itchy night.

The couple decided to go for it, confident that if they headed in what they thought to be south, they would at least come out somewhere on the highway. They reluctantly skied away from their shelter.

Around noon, a team of Search and Rescue snowmobiles intercepted a fresh ski track, but the riders decided to head back to the command post because they had not found any other fresh signs. The searchers knew this area well and decided to "buzz" the shed, just in case. They immediately spotted the fresh ski tracks and knew what they had found. The command post was notified by radio and the riders took off to overtake the skiers.

It only took the riders a few minutes to spot the lost skiers. The skiers had been traveling for over two hours and had gone a couple of miles distance, but they were only about 200 yards, just over the hill and out of sight, from where they had spent the night. Without knowing it, they had made a large sweeping circle ending up almost where they started that morning. They were in excellent condition except for the itching, and ready for a ride home.

This couple had been very fortunate to find the shelter when they did. However, they had been very close to help without realizing it. Every choice of direction they made was exactly wrong. In fact, they had spent the night only 400 yards north of the highway, on the backside of a small tree-covered hill that prevented them from seeing the highway. When they left the shed that morning, had they gone in any direction except the one they had taken, they would have found the highway, ski trail, or help. Additionally, 400 yards to the southwest, over this same hill, was a Colorado Department of Roads maintenance station that had a permanent residence on site. The weather station shed in which they had spent the night was part of the highway department operation, just around a hill out of sight from the other buildings. The hill and the trees had blocked the lights and sounds of the station.

Regardless, the skiers made mistakes before they ever took off. They were in a new area and were over-confident about their abilities. They didn't leave word with anyone about their plans. They didn't inquire about nighttime weather changes. They didn't rely only on the blue ski markers, but followed tracks. They didn't take any fire starters, a compass, extra clothing, or any other precautions to help them if they got into trouble. Before venturing out, it's essential to consider all of the possibilities, and prepare for them as well as you are able.

Clothing

Appropriate clothing and footwear are of primary importance when planning any trip into the wilderness. Do not underestimate how the pain of blisters, a wet head or neck, damp feet, cold hands, or a sunburn can affect your ability to hike or care for yourself. Any of these small problems can quickly escalate into major ones.

Time after time we get calls for an inexperienced cross-country skier who started a tour mid-afternoon when the weather was a calm fifty degrees. They would be dressed for those conditions, then two hours later, when the sun went down and the temperature dropped below freezing, they would be in a life-threatening situation.

Proper clothing is determined by the activity, environmental exposure, and any changes that might occur. Clothing should be adjustable for weather changes and adequately provide protection in any conditions that you may encounter.

The way to make clothing adaptable is to plan in layers. In warmer temperatures, a short-sleeved shirt might be comfortable, but the possibility of sunburn might make long sleeves more appropriate. Mosquitoes, rain, or cooler temperatures might all make you wish for long sleeves. An easy solution is to tie an extra long-sleeved shirt around your waist or carry one in your pack. If temperatures are cool, you might be wearing two shirts and a jacket. When you begin to hike, ski, or otherwise move, you will warm up, and it will be necessary to take off a layer or two to cool down.

Preventing yourself from overheating is just as important as preventing heat loss. If you overheat, you will perspire, which will chill you when you cool back down. In cold temperatures, you do not want your clothing to become damp from perspiration if you can help it. Controlling the moisture your body puts off by wearing layered clothing of appropriate fabrics prevents your clothing from getting wet on the inside.

FABRICS

Cotton. Cotton is one of the most widely used fabrics. It is comfortable, relatively durable, and inexpensive. The biggest problem with cotton is that it loses insulation ability when it becomes wet. There are waterproof coatings that make cotton shed water, but these typically do not hold up very well. Around fire, cotton will burn but not melt to your skin, and it will smolder when in contact with a spark. Cotton is an excellent fabric for warm, drier weather conditions because it is light and breathes well.

Wool. Wool is an excellent natural fiber that provides good insulation when wet or dry. Wool can be dripping wet and it will keep you as warm or warmer than when it is dry.

Wool has some disadvantages, however. It is very itchy when worn in direct contact to your skin, and it shrinks considerably, especially if it is washed in warm or hot water. Wool holds water like a sponge. If you perspire heavily, fall into a creek, or get caught in a rain, you will soon feel like you are carrying an extra hundred pounds. Wool does dry out while you wear it, however, and will keep you warm while it does.

Wool is durable and very reliable. It is bulkier than the newer, high-tech fabrics, but it is still the "old reliable" of fabrics.

Silk. Like wool, silk insulates very well and breathes. The hollow fibers do not trap perspiration next to your skin, so overheating is less of a problem. Silk garments are light and comfortable next to your skin, and being thin and smooth, are great for layering. Washable silk and silk-blend undergarments are available for outdoor recreation, and though initially expensive, silk undergarments will stand up to lots of use.

Polypropylene. Polypropylene is an excellent synthetic fabric that provides insulation wet or dry. It breathes very well, and dries out quickly. It comes in a variety of forms and textures, including some that look and feel like cotton.

I like to wear polypropylene long underwear that looks and feels like a tight cotton sweat suit. You would think it was cotton—except when sparks from a campfire land on it, little melt holes form. Polypropylene has historically had a problem with body odors being trapped in the fibers. It can be washed several times and still retain the odor. Manufacturers have improved the fabric to deal with this problem.

Overall, polypropylene is an excellent fabric for wilderness outings because it dries quickly, maintains heat while wet, is durable, and reasonably priced.

Gore-Tex. The invention of Gore-Tex™ and similar products has revolutionized wilderness clothing. It is probably the most popular windproof, waterproof, yet breathable, fabric on the market. These fabrics allow water vapor but not water droplets to pass through, allowing perspiration to evaporate while keeping out rain.

The disadvantage is that garments are difficult to dry if moisture does get on the inside. The same waterproof feature that keeps water out also keeps it in. Often you must take the garment off and turn it inside out to dry it. Gore-Tex can also be damaged by improper washing, exposure to fuels and chemicals, or by sparks and flame.

When selecting a garment, look at the design. The fabric is waterproof but any stitching, embroidery, zippers, pockets and other features that may make it stylish will also compromise its effectiveness. For example, our rescue group purchased very nice, high-quality Gore-Tex shells for its members, with a very large emblem embroidered on the back. If we were caught in a rain, we stayed very dry except for our backs, which were soaked because the emblem allowed water to penetrate.

Gore-Tex and similar fabrics are highly recommended. They are wind resistant, waterproof, and relatively durable. Garments made from these fabrics are somewhat expensive, but worth the investment.

While it is important to dress in layers and purchase good-quality clothing and jackets made of appropriate materials, there are some low-tech items that are very useful to include in your pack or on your body.

Bandanna. A bandanna is a very useful and versatile item. It can be used as a hat or sweatband, a sling for an injured arm, a pressure bandage for a cut, a tourniquet on a larger wound, or as a washcloth for personal hygiene or to clean a wound.

Spare Socks. Dry, spare socks can be carried in a plastic freezer bag. The bag will keep them dry if you fall in a stream or get your pack wet.

Wet feet become cold more quickly than dry ones, and more likely to develop blisters and problems than dry feet. When you change your socks, dry the wet ones immediately so you will always have a spare pair.

Stocking Cap or Other Hat. If you don't wear a stocking cap, at least carry one in your pack just in case. Hoods on jackets offer great head and neck protection from rain, wind, and snow, but the type of hat that pulls down over the face and neck for added warmth is a small, lightweight addition to your pack that could make a big difference. You can also use the hat as a pad to sit on if you're sitting on a rock or log for a long time.

If you are in sunny conditions, a baseball cap or visor will give your eyes and face some relief from the sun. A baseball cap also keeps the rain from dripping down your face. I also have carried a nylon mask that stretches over the head and face that is designed to fit under a helmet. It is a tight fitting single layer that has holes for your face. This is very lightweight and compact, yet keeps wind directly off your skin.

Gaiters. Gaiters are nylon sleeves that wrap around the upper foot and lower leg to shed water and snow. They are used primarily by cross-country skiers, but are becoming more popular in other winter activities. Gaiters will keep you much drier if you are walking in snow or even wet grass. They offer an inexpensive way to keep your feet and lower pantlegs dry.

Footwear

When selecting footwear, forget style and concentrate on the practical. Boots that fit tightly with oversized heels or tight toes may be practical for horseback riding but are wrong for hiking and other activities. Cowboy boots are designed for a specific function — they fit into a stirrup easily, have a large heel to hold the stirrup in place, and feature a steel shank to support the foot in the middle. Some have a tapered heel designed for coming off a horse and pulling down bulls or other animals. A boot like this is not designed for warmth, walking, or hiking on rough terrain.

You need to protect your feet with well-made, properly fitted boots that match the environment and terrain you'll experience. There are all types of outdoor shoes, from running shoes to felt-lined snowboots. It is not practical to carry extra shoes, so you must choose the best overall shoe for the experience.

One year I hiked into a remote area on an elk hunt. I was wearing good, high quality, felt-lined snow boots that were ideal for snow and some hiking. I hiked into my area, which was about three miles, most of it uphill. My feet were very comfortable during the uphill hike and during the four days I hunted. When it was time to leave, however, I had to hike out the three miles downhill all the way. I had worn the boots for four days, so you would think my feet would have been used to them, but going downhill I soon noticed my feet had a little room to slide forward with each step.

The movement was small, but unavoidable because of the lack of support the boot provided. The boot was designed for warmth and dryness, not rugged hiking. After about a mile, it felt like my toes were curled up in the toe of the boot from constantly sliding forward. The soles of my feet burned from the friction of sliding back and forth over the wool felt. It felt much better on my feet to turn around and walk backward down the trail. It looked a little weird, but it felt better.

This example shows the boot was excellent for the first part of the trip, including the camp but failed walking down hill. Had this failure happened at the beginning of the trip or during a survival situation, I could have had a serious problem. A more appropriate boot would have been a well-made, insulated hiking boot.

There are so many kinds of boots and hiking shoes on the market today that you shouldn't have any trouble finding what you need. Your selection should be determined by the conditions and the intended use. Good quality boots are expensive, but well worth the money. Try the boots on with the same socks and liners you would use outdoors. If you wear more than one layer of socks, or your boots are laced too tightly, you will restrict blood circulation in your feet, making them colder. Extra layers also do not help if the insulation is smashed down tightly. If you plan to use extra socks or moccasins, you must size your boots accordingly.

Your Pack

Assembling your survival pack involves common sense. I have recommended many items; if you were to carry them all, you would need a very large pack. You must try different techniques and develop your own personal pack that works for you.

Do not try to carry too much gear or too little. If your pack is so heavy that it becomes a burden, you will leave it behind. If your pack is too light, you might not have the things you need to survive. Select a model that fits your build, as you will be more likely to carry one that fits.

A first-aid kit and survival kit should be part of your pack, whether it is a smaller day pack for a short hike, or a larger backpack for a trip into the back country. You should also carry a minimum of five fire-starting techniques and suifficient means to purify drinking water. A basic survival kit should be assembled according to your own needs, and carried separately on your person. A few key items can make the difference between life and death.

A small tin box with a tight-fitting lid should contain some or all of the following survival items:

Fishing line and fishing hooks, matches, safety pins, needles and strong thread, a wire saw, small magnifying glass, a small packet of salt (you can become very ill if you do not replace the salt lost through sweat and urine), a strong plastic bag, water sterilizing tablets, adhesive bandages, a small pencil, and a small candle. This tin can be tucked into a pocket or jacket pouch.

WIRE SAW

Around your neck should be at minimum your compass and a whistle. You should also carry a pocketnife in a separate pocket and wear a watch.

Carry your pack anytime that you leave the road. It is a very common mistake to get out of a vehicle, leave the road briefly, spot an interesting object, and walk over to check it out, then be distracted again and suddenly find yourself a distance from your vehicle. Then you determine that going back to the vehicle is too much effort and you only plan to be a few minutes. Accidents can happen anywhere at any time.

One fall day another hunter and I had a couple of elk down and field dressed. We had packed one elk out on horses. On the way to the vehicle with the first load, one of the horses spooked and cut his leg badly. We took the horse to the vet and decided to pack the balance of the meat out by hand, since it was early in the day.

The elk was about a mile off the road on a rugged four-wheel drive road that was blocked by an early snow. While we were in town we picked up

ITEMS TO INCLUDE IN YOUR PACK:

- ☐ *first-aid kit (see p. 105)*
- ☐ *space blanket(s)*
- ☐ *fishing line and hooks*
- ☐ *safety pins*
- ☐ *needles and strong thread*
- ☐ *wire saw*
- ☐ *salt packet or tablets*
- ☐ *strong, large plastic bags*
- ☐ *water-sterilizing tablets*
- ☐ *pencil*
- ☐ *small candle*
- ☐ *flashlight / strobe*

FOR FIRE-STARTING:

- ☐ *matches*
- ☐ *welder's striker*
- ☐ *magnesium shavings*
- ☐ *steel wool and 9V battery*
- ☐ *road flare*
- ☐ *magnifying glass*

AROUND YOUR NECK:

- ☐ *compass*
- ☐ *whistle*

my daughter and the other hunter's sister to help carry out the meat. The other hunter, though a good outdoorsman, was a "flatlander" with no respect for how fast you can get into trouble in the mountains. He ridiculed me, and even got upset, because I insisted on carrying my pack back in to the elk. He figured I could carry much more meat if I wasn't carrying a pack. I didn't listen to him.

Do not let anyone talk you out of carrying your pack. You alone are responsible for your safety. Do not let others influence your good judgment.

The temperature was about twenty-five degrees, calm and sunny. It was a beautiful day. The four of us walked in about three-quarters of a mile where we had to cross a small stream. I didn't notice it, but my daughter slipped on a rock while crossing and filled her boot with water. She didn't say anything at the time, wanting to keep up with the group.

My daughter had only gone about two hundred yards when she was forced to admit what had happened. Her foot was freezing up. A soaked boot has no insulating value; it was draining heat from her body rapidly. She realized her problem and that something had to be done quickly. It had taken only two hundred yards before she couldn't stand it any longer.

There is no way she could have made it back to the vehicle without unnecessary injury.

Since I had brought my pack along, I had a means to start a fire, dry her clothes and boots, and warm her up again. I carried spare socks and made her comfortable very quickly. Don't think a few "I told you so's" weren't going around at the time. It took us about thirty minutes to get her dried out and then we continued down the trail.

The trail followed the stream to where the elk were located, which was on the opposite side of the stream. Instead of everyone crossing the stream, my friend and I decided that we would pack the meat down to this side of the water. We left the two girls and started to cross. While crossing the stream, I slipped, fell backwards and was soaked from head to toe.

I was able to start another fire and dry myself out. I couldn't care less if anyone wants to chuckle at my pack. I will carry it any day, or my daughter will carry it for me.

Maintain your pack. Keep your pack up to date with fresh batteries, fresh food, clean water, or any other items that might deteriorate with time. If you keep candy bars in your pack, keep it secret from your kids or you'll end up like I have on many occasions — a handful of wrappers and a long night.

Become an expert with the equipment you choose. The more you practice, the more comfortable you will be when things get difficult. Experiment with your equipment, testing it to the limits. If you know the failure point of each piece of equipment, you will gain the level of experience and knowledge needed to survive.

Plans

Make a plan and stick to it. When you venture into the wilderness, make sure someone knows your plans. Discuss what that person is to do if you don't return on time, and what you will do if you get hurt or lost. Make your plans specific and follow these plans exactly. Determine how much "cushion time" to allow before someone seeks help. Remember, if no one knows you're missing, no one will be looking for you.

If you change your plans, let someone know! Aircraft pilots follow this procedure by making a flight plan. Before they take off, they call a number, advise the intended route, time of departure and time of arrival. When they arrive, they call back and close the plan. If they do not close the plan, a search is initiated to locate the aircraft. It is not uncommon to initiate a search for an overdue plane just because the pilot landed, got distracted, and forgot to call in.

It is also common for a person to come out of the woods, go to the bar for a few drinks, and stay there until it is quite late. Those at camp or home have no idea where the person is, and assume he or she is stranded and hurt in the freezing cold. They call on Search and Rescue when, in fact, he or she is simply in a Jack Daniel's coma in a nice warm bar. If someone is expecting you, call them if you will be late. A lot of unnecessary energy and searching takes place just because people don't inform those who expect them.

Make a plan and stick to it. When you venture into the wilderness, make sure someone knows your plans. Determine how much "cushion time" to allow before someone seeks help.

Developing Your Survival Skills

I have recommended many items in writing this information. I hope you have picked up on the concept that survival skills are basically new thinking, planning and practice. No book or conversation will substitute for hands-on experience. You must try each technique and see if it will work for you. If you can't make things work right in a controlled setting, you will not be able to do so in poor conditions. If you can't build a fire in your fireplace or in a campfire, you will not be able to build one in the rain, snow, or wind.

Your mind is the most powerful asset you possess in a life-threatening situation. When things are relaxed and controlled, sit and think of survival situations and then think of how you would deal with those problems. Test the solutions you come up with and see if they really work. If you have found the solution difficult in practice, it will become impossible in reality. If you find solutions that work, they will come naturally when the problems happen in a real setting.

Your mental and physical preparation along with the proper equipment and experience will provide you with highest possible chance of survival when things get difficult. Mental preparation will give you a positive mental attitude, believing that you can and will survive.

Index